ROAST
of the
TOWN

ROAST
of the
TOWN

—

JOEY ADAMS

—

PRENTICE HALL PRESS
New York

Published by Prentice Hall Press
A Division of Simon & Schuster, Inc.
Gulf + Western Building
One Gulf + Western Plaza
New York, NY 10023

PRENTICE HALL PRESS is a trademark of Simon & Schuster, Inc.

Library of Congress Cataloging-in-Publication Data
Adams, Joey, 1911–
Roast of the town.
   1. Invective—Anecdotes, facetiae, satire, etc.
I. Title.
PN6231.I65A33   1986   818'.5402   86-9370

ISBN 0-13-781436-4

Manufactured in the United States of America

10 9 8 7 6 5 4 3 2 1

First Edition

CONTENTS

PART I

The Gentle Art of Insult

The Roast of the Town

In this era of masochistic comedy, our most famous person-alities have accepted testimonials in their honor, just to be carved to pieces by their "friends" and associates.

To be part of this new school of dais assassins, you must adhere to the motto "If you can't say anything nice about the guy—let's hear it."

The "honored" one is sworn to take it. The big question is, can you give it? That's what I'm here for—to arm you with the appropriate ammunition.

The idea is to use a joke instead of a stick, a gag instead of a rock—a laugh instead of a bomb.

Laugh and the world laughs with you; cry and it means you can't take it—or, worse, you can't dish it out. Jokes are the strongest weapons you can use, and laughter is the great-est defense.

Nobody laughed harder than RONALD REAGAN when I said at one dinner: "What's the big deal about a man of his age being President? About the only job a seventy-four-year-old man can get in this country is President of the United States."

The Prez not only took it, he returned it: "That JOEY ADAMS knows a lot—he just can't think of it."

Poor JIMMY CARTER, he just couldn't take the heat—or the joke. If I did a joke in my column, "Strictly for Laughs," about any of the Carters, the White House was ready to kill. All I said was "Amy is taking skiing lessons because she wants to go downhill with her father." The next day I got a call from Washington: "Why are you picking on the President of the United States?"

I said on the air, "President Carter says his anti-inflation program is working—the trouble is the people aren't." The next call from the White House said, "The President is distraught—what are you trying to prove?"

All I said was "I'm trying to prove that the President has a sense of humor like a dunked tea bag."

If you're going out for public office, you have to be able to take it as well as throw it—and nobody throws it better than RONALD REAGAN.

When I said, "Why do they say Reagan is too old to run for President of the United States? Just because his social security number is two?" R.R. called personally: "Joey, this is Ron!" I said, "Ron, I'm busy—what is it?" He laughed. "What kind of lousy joke is that—my social security number is two?" I said, "You got a better one? He said, "Sure—why do they say I'm too old to be President? Just because my social security number is in Roman numerals."

It was my "adopted father," the late Mayor of New York, FIORELLO LA GUARDIA, who first taught me how to turn chaos into harmony with one twist of humor. When one of his appointees stole some money, Fiorello went on the air and took full responsibility: "I very seldom make a mistake—but when I do it's a beaut." The laughter proved all was forgiven, and the line became such a part of the language that we've forgotten who said it first.

In JOHN F. KENNEDY's case, humor was an integral part of his image. His humor helped establish a national mood—and it got him out of a lot of trouble.

When he became President, one of his first appointments was BOBBY KENNEDY, his kid brother, as attorney general. Bobby was only just out of law school—I think he was about eleven years old—and everybody screamed nepotism. I saw the President before he held his press conference, and suggested the line that laughed him out of it.

One reporter started: "How could you appoint a young boy, just out of law school, as attorney general of the most powerful country in the world?"

The Prez smiled. "Well, he's my kid brother, and I wanted to give him *some* experience before he opened his own law office." Everybody howled and the problem was over—J.F.K. had laughed himself well again.

That's the idea of this book: to prepare you for battle, to arm you with jokes, gags, stories, anecdotes, and answers in case you run into a heckler, a dais full of murderers, a toast-master with a scalpel, or any group not especially friendly to what you've got to say.

Insults and Roasts

If the butcher, the baker, the plumber, or the comic is trying to beat you to the punch line, you will now be ready. Insults are a way of life—without them you couldn't talk to HENNY YOUNGMAN or DON RICKLES; wives couldn't describe their spouses. If you didn't have insults, how would you be able to refer to KHADAFY, ARAFAT, or the lovable AYATOLLAH? Herewith some samples of the genteel wit of insult—otherwise known as the roast.

JOAN RIVERS has a black belt in mouth. The trouble with Joan is, she can't cook but she likes to dish it out.

CASTRO is all for peace—he'll bury the hatchet . . . in anybody.

DEAN MARTIN drinks to steady his nerves. The other night he got so steady he couldn't move.

JACKIE GLEASON drinks to pass the time. Last night he passed 1955.

GEORGE BURNS is at the age when his sex drive is in park.

STOCKBROKER: He's an unhappy broker—he's got a dozen stocks that went bad—and a secretary who didn't.

WIFE: She's a magician—she can turn anything into an argument.

HUSBAND: He owes a lot to his country, and the I.R.S. will catch up someday. He lost control of his car the other day—he forgot to make the payments.

MOTHER-IN-LAW: People could listen to her for hours, and they *have* to.

TV REPAIRMAN: When he went on jury duty, they found him guilty.

RODNEY DANGERFIELD: Even when he was a kid they knew he'd go far—they chased him.

TIP O'NEILL got carried away with his own importance—but not far enough.

JESSE JACKSON: People like to help him out—as soon as he comes in.

DON RICKLES is an angry man—he goes to a fortune-teller to have his fist read.

BUTCHER: He works to keep his hand in—the cash register.

BANKER: He's helped people run their fortune into a shoestring.

MANUFACTURER: He pays his bills with a smile—most of his creditors would prefer cash.

MAILMAN: He's a nice fella but he doesn't make house calls.

ACTOR: He's glad he's got a split personality—so he can date himself.

PLAYGIRL: She has the gift of grab.

FEMALE POLITICIAN: She isn't running for office—but her seat is up for sale.

CONGRESSMAN: He can talk for two hours on any given subject—four hours if he knows anything about it.

Insults are now a big business. Every politician and civilian is asking me for zingers to lay on their friends, the manufacturers (doctors, lawyers, plumbers) who are having a dinner in their honor a week from Thursday. Be my guest . . . Who was the first celebrity to be roasted? Joan of Arc.

NERD: I don't want to say this guy is tacky, but the airlines all refuse to sell him a first-class ticket. He's a man who has no equals—only superiors.

LAWYER: This man doesn't have an enemy in the world—and none of his friends like him. He has an unlisted phone, a numbered bank account, and a post office mailing address—which is all unnecessary, because nobody wanted to reach him in the first place. He loves to listen when money talks. He guarantees that if you go to jail, he will take care of your wife's sexual needs.

ACTOR: He's very well known. He's been written up many times—he's got ninety-eight parking tickets—and he is deeply religious—he worships himself.

ACCOUNTANT: His father used to play games with him, like throwing him in the air—then walking away.

GAMBLER: He's got property in Las Vegas—he left two of his bags at Caesar's Palace.

LOVER: He was making love to his wife and she lost her place in her book *twice.*

"It's gonna be a real battle of wits," HENNY YOUNGMAN told me. "How brave of you," I said, "to go into battle unarmed." That's what I'm doing here—arming you with a first-aid kit of punchlines.

I said to HENNY: "You have a ready wit—I'll let you know when it's ready."

I said to a former friend: "I never forget a face. In your case, I'll remember both of them."

To your BOOKMAKER: "It's good to see you—it means you're not behind my back."

About the **BOSS**: His motto is "a tooth for a tooth"—but he expects yours to have gold in them.

DOCTOR: He's in danger of losing his license for having made love to his patients; it's a damn shame, because he's the best veterinarian in town. It's not true he'll sell his own grandmother—renting is as far as he'll go. He owns a chain of homes for unwed mothers called "All the Way House." He's always been a big help to people—so has Kaopectate. I found a way to get my doctor to make house calls—I bought a home on the golf course. He is working on what could be the biggest advance in medical history—billing you even before you get sick. A patient came in with walking pneumonia and he charged her by the mile.

POLITICIAN: He's such a dumb politician—he lost the election when he asked Greenwich Village voters to follow a straight ticket. Now take **TIP O'NEILL**—*please*; he never met a cake he didn't like. I promised to announce that **WALTER MONDALE** wanted to be remembered—by anybody. An open mind is a wonderful thing—as long as a matching mouth doesn't always go with it. He's the kind of guy who could brighten up anyone's day—just by saying good-bye.

BUSINESSMAN: Maybe there's some hope for him—now that they've developed an artificial heart. Some businessman: He represents **YASIR ARAFAT** for shaving commercials.

STOCKBROKER: What's it like doing business with him? Some guys named their first ulcers after him.

He willed his body to science and science contested the will.

ENGINEER: His life is so dull, he actually looks forward to dental appointments.

SECRETARY: She knows all the answers—but nobody asks her the questions.

DISK JOCKEY: He's the only radio personality who leaves the studio in a getaway car!

BARTENDER: I may not agree with what you say—but I'll defend to the death your right to shut up!

PRODUCER: He's working on a new book, *The Joy of Cheap.*

YOUR NEIGHBOR: He's not such a bad guy—until you get to know him.

TO CRANKY CAB DRIVER: "Do you have a chip on your shoulder, or is that your head?"

ACTOR: His wife just uncovered a new stack of love letters—that he wrote to himself.

About PHYLLIS DILLER: They caught a peeping Tom outside her bedroom window—sleeping.

STEVE ALLEN: When I can't sleep I read a book by STEVE ALLEN.

JOAN RIVERS: Joan was happy and went to see her doctor—he gave her a shot of venom, and she felt like herself again. When she got married, nobody would give the bride away—they finally held an auction.

JOHNNY CARSON: A man like him is hard to find—to find him we had to look in three bars and a massage parlor.

Sooner or later everybody—my doctor, my lawyer, my congressman, my doorman—everybody comes to me for jokes. Sooner or later everybody has to make some speech—even if it's only to dump on your best friend who just got a raise or lost his job or his wife. That's the reason for this book—to prepare you for everything but failure.

Our guest of honor just got back from a short vacation—for a couple of days last week, he took leave of his senses. Our honored guest is a humble and modest man—and with good reason. To him, a woman's body is a temple—and he tries to attend services as often as possible. I can honestly say that in all the years I've known him, no one ever questioned his intelligence—in fact, I never heard anyone mention it.

Self-depreciation often gets the biggest laughs. It's still the roast, still insult humor, but with the speaker as his own target.

JOAN RIVERS: "Thirteen is unlucky for me—it's my bust size."

MILTON BERLE: "My wallet's full of big bills—I wish some of them were paid."

RICH LITTLE: "I once filled in for ailing DOLLY PARTON in Las Vegas—thank God I only had to fill her shoes."

Are you roasting the stars?

ELIZABETH TAYLOR ran out of men—she started marrying men she had already married.

ED McMAHON: It's obvious Ed's importance is limited to JOHNNY CARSON—when JOANNA filed for divorce, the only thing she *didn't* ask for was McMahon!

GEORGE BURNS always wanted to learn. As a boy he read everything that Shakespeare wrote—but then, when he was a boy Shakespeare hadn't written much.

JOHNNY CARSON: To most girls he's a father figure—they keep asking him for money.

GEORGE STEINBRENNER can be outspoken—but I've never seen anybody do it.

To attorney ROY COHN's credit, he can be tolerant of people who disagree with him—he feels everyone is entitled to his own stupid opinion.

MUHAMMAD ALI has never said an unkind word about anybody—that's because he never talks about anybody but himself.

Laugh Yourself Well

NORMAN COUSINS was at my birthday party and suggested that the nicest present my friends could give me was a good gag, joke, or belly laugh. It was Norman Cousins who really encouraged me to write this book: "Your jokes, columns, and books helped save my life," he told me. "My doctor said that a Joey Adams joke before or after medication—or instead— would help me laugh myself well.' "

That's why this book of roasts. A dose of joy is a spiritual cure. And since there is no such thing as gentle humor, *let's roast the hell out of them.*

GEORGE BURNS wrote: "In your youth you liked wine, women and song—thank God you can still sing."

CARY GRANT noted: "When people tell you how young you look, they are also telling you how old you are."

GEORGE CARLIN's present: *"Don't pray on Monday.* The Muslim sabbath is Friday, the Jewish sabbath is Saturday, the Christian sabbath is Sunday—on Monday God is hung over."

BETTE DAVIS's gift: "I never trust an overly modest man—a guy failing to toot his own horn may simply have a dead battery."

JACKIE MASON taught: "Did you know in my religion the sin of eating bread on Passover is comparable to the sin of adultery? I told this to a friend and he says he tried them both and can't see the comparison."

ANTHONY QUINN wired: "Middle age is when you have more fun remembering what you did than what you're doing."

Congressman **MARIO BIAGGI** said: "Congress is the first nuthouse I've ever known that's run by the inmates."

BOB HOPE submitted: "You know you're getting old when everything you own is paid for and and you can finally afford all the things you no longer want."

MARLON BRANDO cabled: "A fat man will never look old—there's no room for wrinkles."

WARREN BEATTY suggested: "Designer jeans prices are ridiculous. If I spend $75 for a pair of jeans, I expect a woman to be in them."

MILTON BERLE: "I'm at the age now when if a girl flirts with me in the movies, she's after my popcorn."

DEBORAH RAFFIN said: "Some girls are music lovers—I can love without it."

BARBRA STREISAND: "Would you believe **LIBERACE** is afraid of the dark—when he goes to sleep he leaves his jacket lit."

GENE BAYLOS: "Our TV man had to take our set back to the store for an adjustment—it needed back payments."

ELIZABETH TAYLOR said she called up her bridesmaids: "It's time to get back to work."

MICKEY ROONEY wired me: "One thing, there are no hookers working Rodeo Drive—hookers here don't accept MasterCard."

MAYOR KOCH sent a letter instead of a telegram: "New York is strapped for cash—maybe we should have the streetwalkers double as meter maids."

I'm not too anxious to admit it, but other people sometimes say funny things, too.

JAN MURRAY said it: "I once suffered from senility—but I forgot about it."

RONALD REAGAN: "The White House gets about 120,000 letters a week from the post office. Unfortunately, most of them are addressed to Calvin Coolidge."

Moses had the right idea—he only wrote one-liners. Of course, he only wrote ten. It's taken us a couple of thousand years, but we got a few more now: If you can't give up sex, get married and taper off. Nine times out of ten, if somebody gives you the business, it's probably failing. Early to bed and early to rise is a sure sign you're fed up with TV.

Celebrity one-liners are always devastating.

BETTE MIDLER: "PRINCESS ANNE of England is such an active lass, so outdoorsy—she loves nature in spite of what it did to her."

TWIGGY asks, "What are the two greatest reasons for DOLLY PARTON's rise to stardom?"

JOE NAMATH: "MICKEY ROONEY's favorite exercise is climbing tall people."

When it comes to show people, the "I's" have it. They must talk about themselves—even if it means putting themselves down.

PHYLLIS DILLER: "The only man who thinks I'm a ten is my shoe salesman."

RODNEY DANGERFIELD: "I admit I'm not too bright—it takes me an hour and a half to watch *Sixty Minutes*."

ANTHONY QUINN: "The reason I have such a good memory for names is because I took that Sam Carnegie course."

In this age of instant coffee and frozen TV dinners, who's got time for long drawn-out stories; you've got to do it all in one-liners:

It's always darkest before the light bill is paid. Cleanliness is next to godliness—in the Bronx it's next to impossible. If the early bird catches the worm, why doesn't the dumb worm stay in bed?

Hateful thoughts for happy occasions:

"No wonder we love each other—who else could stand us?" "Darling, you'll go far—why not leave right now?" "I'm not much to look at—at least we have *that* in common."

"Say the words that will make me the happiest man in the world—'I'm leaving.' " "You came to me from out of no-where—go back."

"You look like a million bucks—all wrinkled and green."

Signs tell a whole story quickly:

Sign in bra shop: WE FIX FLATS. Barbershop: YOUR HAIRCUT IS FREE IF I TALK FIRST. Chicken farm: EGGS LAID WHILE YOU WAIT. Tailor shop: I AM A MAN OF THE CLOTH. Bookstore: HOW I BEAT THE INCOME TAX—BY #36954321. Law office: IF YOU DON'T HAVE

15

ULCERS, YOU'RE NOT CARRYING YOUR SHARE OF THE LOAD. Pawnshop: PLEASE SEE ME AT YOUR EARLIEST INCONVENIENCE.

Chinese fortune cookies tell the whole story in one little cracker:

"Never start argument with wife when she is tired—or when she is rested." "He love her like anything—and he love anything." "Better late than audited." "A man is known by the company he thinks nobody knows he's keeping." "Help preserve wild life—throw a party tonight." "Showing someone the ropes is a good way to hang yourself."

Now for the comics:

MILTON BERLE: "If you want to forget your troubles, wear tight shoes."

BOB HOPE: "In Moscow I was given the keys *out* of the city."

GEORGE BURNS: "With all the body parts available these days, you don't have to worry about dying—only rusting." "A miracle cure is anything that's paid for by Medicare."

WOODY ALLEN notes: "New York State has a very funny law that says you can't get a divorce unless you can prove adultery, and that's strange because the Ten Commandments say 'Thou shall not commit adultery.' So New York State says you *have* to."

LUCILLE BALL says: "It's no wonder a woman's work is never done. Just about the time she thinks it is, she becomes a grandmother." "Girls used to show a lot of style—today's styles show a lot of girl." "New York, New York, it's a wonderful town. We've got equipment to tow away your car—but nothing to tow away the garbage."

ALAN KING says: "Today a good diplomat must speak a number of languages—including double talk." "PRESIDENT REAGAN is right. We got to protect our interest in Latin America. Why, right now some of those countries are so mad at us, they won't even give us receipts when they take our money."

JERRY LEWIS checked in with: "When an Arab oil sheikh was leaving for a trip to the U.S., his wife told him to bring her back a little something cute in silk—so he brought her three jockeys from Aqueduct."

My story of the year is about the couple registering at a small hotel in Vermont. The clerk asked them to show their wedding license. The man flashed a fishing license to the nearsighted clerk and laid it on the table. After the couple went upstairs the clerk examined the license more carefully and rushed up after them. He banged on the door, shouting: "If you ain't done it, don't do it; this ain't the license for it!"

EARL WILSON notes: "There are so many sex magazines on the newsstands, I'm taking a course in speed looking."

More "Earl's Pearls": "Punk was invented so ugly kids could be popular too." Hollywood's gag of the year was told by gays about gays and they took responsibility for it: "Three guys attacked a woman in Beverly Hills. Two held her down and one did her hair."

Now, here are the ten greatest one-liners since the ten that Moses brought down:

1. CARY GRANT: "Divorce is a game played by lawyers."

2. BO DEREK: "Whoever said money can't buy happiness didn't know where to shop."

3. ZSA ZSA GABOR: "The most popular labor-saving device is still a husband with money."

4. ALAN KING: "If you want to read about love and marriage, you've got to buy two separate books."

5. HENRY KISSINGER: "Ninety percent of the politicians give the other ten percent a bad name."

6. BOB HOPE: "A penny saved is worthless."

7. JOHNNY CARSON: "Support free enterprise—legalize prostitution."

8. MARILYN MONROE: "Before marriage a girl has to make love to her man to hold him; after marriage she has to hold him to make love to him."

9. ELIZABETH TAYLOR: "I've only slept with men I've been married to. How many woman can make that statement?"

10. DOLLY PARTON: "The night of our honeymoon my husband took one look and said, 'Is that all for me?'"

Prepared for Battle

My prescription for laughter is to supply you with jokes, gags, punch lines, and roast lines for any and all occasions.

Here are some loving put-downs for those of you who come to roast or even to electrocute. Use them to fit your target—to light the bomb under some poor suspecting guest:

He opened a halfway house for girls who couldn't go all the way.

He never gives up. He's still holding an IOU from Judge Crater.

A priest should be allowed to get married and find out what hell really is.

He has never been bored himself—but he is a carrier.

He can get any girl he pleases. Up to now he hasn't pleased any.

He's in the same condition as the Great Wall of China—stoned.

I have not known our guest of honor long, but I know him as long as I intend to.

Our guest of honor is a man who, ever since he's been old enough to work, hasn't.

Nothing is impossible for the executive who doesn't have to do it himself.

He goes with this girl, Sylvia. Everybody says she's a ten, but I happen to know she charges twenty.

Are you facing a roomful of doctors? "It's true a doctor will always take care of poor people, even if it means making you one." "I was a little upset when my doctor charged me $500 and told me I'm going to have to live with it. That's like a hooker telling you to take a cold shower."

Is a dentist your guest of honor? "The modern dentist lives up to his claim: It won't hurt a bit—until the bill comes." I said to my dentist, "You may be a painless dentist, but this is going to hurt a little. I don't have the money."

Is it a dinner for a bunch of bankers? "The same guy that writes the advertising for the bank is not the same guy that gives you the loan."

Is it a church affair? "My wife is so Catholic we can't get fire insurance—too many candles in the house."

A charity dinner? "A philanthropist is a guy who gives away publicly what he stole personally."

Is it a labor rally? "I have always found that a good labor

leader is the kind of guy who believes that a kind word and a kick in the ass are always better than just a kind word."

Is it a PTA meeting? "Slap your child at least once a day. If you don't know why, he does."

The busiest at these dinners is the roastmaster, the hangman who has vowed to dishonor the guest—or guests. I always let my fellow sharpshooters know where I'm aiming with my introduction of our honored guest.

At the March of Dimes roast for JERRY LEWIS, I drew first blood: "We have toasted the who's who of show business at our annual dinners, but this year we looked to top it. We wanted to honor the most beloved of all entertainers—but BOB HOPE didn't want it, DEAN MARTIN said, 'Shove it,' MILTON BERLE said, 'Stick it,' so we got him—JERRY LEWIS."

I introduced JOHNNY CARSON at a show-business dinner for the Actors Youth Fund: "Every once in a while Broadway comes to its senses and honors a man that deserves it—a man of talent, integrity, sincerity. Unfortunately, this isn't the time. Instead we honor Johnny Carson."

JOEY BISHOP honored PHIL SILVERS: "For years the Friars have always roasted the ones we love. Today we break that tradition in honoring Phil Silvers."

That's the idea of this book—to get you ready for all the wars. I even stole, I mean lifted, that is, borrowed some of these lines to help you become the knife of the party.

A plumber can't work without his tools—what is Liberace

without his teeth, or Liz Taylor without a husband? And think of the case of DOLLY PARTON.

You sometimes hear a person say that he will speak "off the cuff," impromptu. But the term *off the cuff* originally meant that the speaker had prepared himself, at least to some extent, by making notes on his shirt cuff, notes that he could easily read without seeming to.

I used to write my notes on my shirt cuff myself. However, I stopped when I heard my laundryman on the Johnny Carson show one night, doing my whole act. He was a big hit, too.

No matter what your handicaps are as a speaker, they will be increased a hundredfold if you are not thoroughly prepared. If you are, many of your supposed handicaps will disappear. Don't rely on inspiration—ever. Be prepared, or prepare to run.

I once introduced BOB HOPE at a Boy Scout luncheon with a glowing eulogy that even he didn't believe. "After such an introduction," he said modestly, "I can hardly wait to hear what I have to say." But even the itinerant Hope wouldn't be so cockily confident if he weren't prepared for battle. All I'm trying to tell you is that you've got to do your homework if you want to pass the exam.

You have my permission to steal, I mean borrow, any of these jokes, gags, or roast lines. In fact, you have my plea—spread the laughs around:

JACKIE VERNON says: "A guy becomes a comedian the way a girl becomes a prostitute. First he does it for fun, then for a few friends, and finally he figures he might as well get paid for it."

I always feel at home when I'm being roasted, and there's always some comic in residence at the Friars Club to make me feel at home. "I never miss your columns in the *Post*," **BUDDY HACKETT** said to me at a lunch. "I never see it so I never miss it."

MILTON BERLE welcomed me: "You're my favorite comedian, second only to **ARAFAT**."

DON RICKLES was sweet: "Joey has always been a big help to people. So has milk of magnesia."

SAMMY CAHN said: "You're OK in my book, but I only read dirty books."

SOUPY SALES sat down to be friendly: "I hear you're writing a new book called *The Joy of Cheap*. It's been so long since you paid for anything, you still don't know prices have gone up."

RED BUTTONS embraced me: "I hear your wife had a mirror installed over your bed because she likes to watch herself laugh." **MICKEY ROONEY** interrupted: "At least he gives his wife something to live for—a divorce."

BOB HOPE: "Someday Joey will go too far—and I hope he stays there."

In the old days, the Indians used to burn you at the stake if they didn't like you. Today at the Friars they roast you alive if they *do* like you.

Chief Throwing Bull is **MILTON BERLE**: "**JOEY ADAMS** is a man about whom much has been written—but very little has been read." "**HENNY YOUNGMAN** is so cheap, he's got the first penny ever thrown at him." "JERRY LEWIS is a good egg—and you know where eggs come from."

Uncle Miltie embraced DON RICKLES: "When they made Don, they threw away the shovel." "They told me to say two words about BUDDY HACKETT. How about *short* and *cheap*."

"HOWARD COSELL had an unhappy childhood. When he was five he ran away from home, and when the police came, his parents couldn't describe him."

Milton fried MICKEY ROONEY at one Friars roast: "He was an ugly kid. He went to parties and played spin the bottle. If you didn't want to kiss anybody you had to give him a quarter. Would you believe, by the time he was twelve years old he owned his own house."

Recently, the big guns were turned on pussycat Berle. FRANK SINATRA figured it wasn't necessary to give him a hand when a finger would do: "I've known Milton a lifetime and he's been making audiences laugh for thirty years. Unfortunately, he's been in business sixty years."

Once I boldly told Milton I loved him, but he *is* conceited. He shouted, "*Me* conceited? The Great Berle?"

Everybody likes to return the compliment to DON RICKLES. SINATRA: "What can you say about Don that hasn't been said about warts." BOB HOPE: "It was Don who taught the Arabs how to fight dirty." ALAN KING: "Don was born at home—but when his mother saw him she went to the hospital."

Take These Ad Libs—Please

SAYINGS OF THE STARS

JOAN RIVERS asked ELIZABETH TAYLOR. "Do you think I'm conceited?" Liz said, "No, why do you ask?" "Because most people who are as attractive, intelligent, and witty as I am usually are conceited." Liz said, "Next to GERALDINE FERRARO, you're still the funniest."

MERV GRIFFIN said, "That DEAN MARTIN never has a hangover—he stays drunk."

FRANK SINATRA praised ROBERT REDFORD: "He has finally found his true love—too bad he can't marry himself."

JACK CARTER said: "Even on the phone RODNEY DANGER-FIELD gets no respect. Last week he called up for the right time—the recording hung up on him."

MOREY AMSTERDAM said: "If ERNEST BORGNINE lost face, it would be an improvement."

DON RICKLES, the merchant of venom, maligns everybody

equally: "EDDIE FISHER was once married to ELIZABETH TAYLOR—that's like trying to wash down the Statue of Liberty with one bar of soap." "I understand that MERV GRIFFIN went to Israel recently and sold them the rights to the perfect bomb—his television show." "BOB NEWHART is a shy guy. His wife had to postpone their honeymoon until she could explain to him what it was."

At a recent roast in Rickles's dishonor, we all returned the compliment. MILTON BERLE said, "He was a very ugly kid. Every time his father wanted to make love to his mother, she would show him a picture of Don."

FRANK SINATRA: "Rickles would make a perfect stranger."

ROBERT REDFORD: "Underneath Rickles's rough exterior there really is a rabid shark."

JACK CARTER: "You very seldom see Don at parties—he's usually busy walking his pet rat."

BOB HOPE: "There's one thing that can be said about Don Rickles—but I don't use that kind of language."

BUDDY HACKETT: "Rickles is the only man I know who has a film of the attack on Pearl Harbor with a laugh track."

The greatest compliment I received from Buddy: "Reading Joey's new book is like making love to your own wife—you want to get it over as quick as you can without looking at it too much."

JOHNNY CARSON: "ARAFAT is so depressed he's been hanging around the house clean-shaven."

Berle to PHYLLIS DILLER: "If you were the only girl in the world, you'd still have trouble."

JOAN RIVERS, the mouth that roared, makes Don Rickles sound like a choirboy: "**NANCY REAGAN** has bulletproof hair—if they ever combed it, they'd find **JIMMY HOFFA**." "**BO DEREK** is gorgeous, but not the brightest—she studies for a Pap test."

SOUPY SALES said to **JERRY LEWIS**: "Why don't you put your face in dough and make jackass cookies?"

GENE BAYLOS is a low-profile type. Before his wife lets him in the bed at night, he has to show his American Express card."

BOB HOPE does it to himself: "I thank my family for keeping me going and my barber for keeping me from looking like I went."

Don Rickles said to **JOHNNY CARSON**, "Laugh it up, hockey puck, you're making $50 million a year and your darling folks in Nebraska are eating locusts for dinner."

DEAN MARTIN said, "Don was so ugly when he was born that the doctor slapped his mother instead of him."

BOB NEWHART'S squelch: "You don't have any brothers, Don, because your mother took one look at you and said, 'Never again.' "

They say that drinking interferes with your sex life, but **DEAN MARTIN** figures it's the other way around.

GEORGE BURNS is always looking for younger woman. At his age, there's no such thing as an older woman.

MICKEY ROONEY about a comic: "He's not too swift. He's the kind of guy who would steal a car and keep up the payments."

Don Rickles about President RONALD REAGAN: "I would never insult a President of the United States. I'm happy to see one of FRANK SINATRA's friends making it."

About BOB NEWHART: "The only reason Bob Newhart and I are such good friends is that he's good at adding restaurant checks and I'm good at being funny."

About FRANK SINATRA: "Frank Sinatra and I are such good friends that he always makes me walk in front of him if we're in a big crowd or heavy traffic."

About DEAN MARTIN: "I once asked Dean Martin, 'What kind of person are you?' and he answered, 'I don't know, because nobody's told me.' "

About GEORGE BURNS: "At his age you've got to humor George Burns. So I let him set fire to my pants. Also, I get him a prune juice fix twice a day."

To JOHNNY CARSON: "I really like your show. I use it as a night-light."

To Don's nightclub audience: "FRANK SINATRA couldn't be here tonight. He's posing for a postage stamp."

To HARRY JAMES: "Too bad your lip is gone. Can you hum?"

To WAYNE NEWTON: "Wayne, I've seen you in nightclubs, I've watched you in movies, I've listened to your records, and I say this from my heart: You're dull."

Seeing TONY CURTIS in his audience: "I remember Tony when all he did was run around with a sword, dueling. In those days his Bronx accent was so bad it embarrassed his butcher."

You can use the answers of the celebrities and apply them to your own target.

JACKIE GLEASON: "Don Rickles has all the charm of an earthquake. Every night he puts out the cat—with ether."

DEAN MARTIN: "Don Rickles is the greatest comic in the world. He is the funniest and nicest man I know. But you know, I'm drunk, and when I'm drunk I'm the biggest liar in the world."

JACK CARTER: "Don's the kind of guy that would buy his mother a swimming pool in Florida and put sharks in it."

JOHNNY CARSON: "Don Rickles will always work—if there's no one else around with talent."

A lot of stars were happy to sign their names to a toast or roast of HOWARD COSELL.

WOODY ALLEN: "When you have dinner with him, he broadcasts the meal."

LILLIAN CARTER: "I don't want him to die, but I wish they'd take him off the air."

DICK CAVETT: "He once walked around with a harpoon sticking out of him for two weeks without noticing it."

HOWARD COSELL: "Arrogant, pompous, obnoxious, vain, cruel, persecuting, distasteful, verbose, a show-off. I have been called all of these. Of course, I am."

JOE NAMATH: "He's the kind of guy who, when he meets

someone, says very loudly, 'This must be a great day for you—meeting me.' "

JOE GARAGIOLA: "He's so nauseatingly gratuitous, going that extra step—including in language, which he cripples while believing he's advancing it."

RED BUTTONS: "He can remember the night he lost his innocence in the back seat of the family car. It would have been even more memorable if he hadn't been alone."

JOHN SIMON: "There is nothing about the work of Howard Cosell to convince us that he has ever felt humility or love anywhere—except in front of a mirror."

And now for the master. MILTON BERLE said to HOWARD COSELL: "You know, I'm forming an attachment for you. It fits right over your mouth."

To BUDDY HACKETT: "You're a real magician—you just made an ass of yourself."

About GENE BAYLOS: "He's a man who really got it all together—unfortunately, he forgot where he put it. The only thing that can stay in his head more than an hour is a cold. If he said what he thought, he'd be speechless."

"HENNY YOUNGMAN would be more popular if he were as well known as his jokes. The greatest form of flattery is imitation, and one of Henny's unusual traits is that he is flattered by the fact that for many years he has been an imitation of a comedian."

Milton Berle loves to praise me: "Your book, Joey Adams, makes a great book for gift-giving—it beats reading it yourself. I like your book—the pages are softer than Charmin. I got my copy for free—and I still feel cheated."

Milton spares nobody. Don't try to stop Milton Berle—just memorize. I go back a long way with Milton, and his jokes go back even further: "Do you know what it means to come home to a woman who'll give you a little love, a little affection, a little tenderness? It means you're in the wrong house. It takes my wife forty minutes to get her lipstick on. You know why? Because she's got a big mouth, that's why."

Milton Berle opened and closed in a show called *Good-night Grandpa.* After the reviews, it was good-bye *Grandpa,* but not good-bye Berle. Milton beat everybody to the laughs. Although he had roasted many, he was now able to roast himself as well: "They gave the author a twenty-one-gun salute—unfortunately, they missed. What can you expect? We opened under great difficulties—the curtain was up. It wasn't easy doing a show in that theater," he explained, "the seats faced the stage."

The Friars finally got a chance to give it to the roastmaster himself: Why not? He's been giving it to us for years. I started the assassination: "Milton, in my book you're a great guy—but then, it's a work of fiction."

BOB HOPE: "A comedian is a man who originates old jokes—Berle is a guy who knows a good gag when he steals one. And Berle is the hottest act in town—every part is stolen."

STEVE ALLEN: "Berle is a great comic. After all, he's been on TV for years, and I finally figured out the reason for his success—he's never improved."

HENNY YOUNGMAN hollered out: "Milton, you got a great delivery—it belongs on a truck."

HENNY added: "Let's show our sympathy for Milton—he just had a charisma bypass."

JAN MURRAY was very kind. "Milton was abandoned by wolves and reared by his parents," Jan screamed. "His parents hated him—when he was four years old, his mother and father were still trying to get an abortion." Jan added, "But he's a good guy—he's really a humanitarian. He'll help anybody—so does the Heimlich maneuver."

NORM CROSBY noted, "You hear about all the Hollywood sex scandals out there—and we can all sleep better, knowing that our guest of honor is physically incapable of sexual scandal."

RED BUTTONS was loving: "I'd rather spend fifteen minutes in this man's company than seven weeks in a hospital." Red reminded us that Berle is into international politics: "He just sent a get-well card to GORBACHEV—he figured, why wait till the last minute."

Roasting Yourself for Fun and Profit

Roasting is not necessarily an act of homicide—in some cases it can be an act of suicide. Some of our biggest stars have become rich and famous by putting themselves down:

PHYLLIS DILLER doesn't wait for anybody to roast her—she does it to herself. "I'm like no other woman in the world. For one thing, my legs don't match. Another thing," Phyllis admits, "I'm the only girl I know that wears prescription underwear." Our gal says: "If my jeans could talk, they'd plead for mercy." She claims, "I walked into a psychiatrist's office. The doc took one look at me and said, 'Get *under* the couch.'"

Phyllis's looks are legendary. When she first decided to go into show business, her looks helped her get her foot in the door—the rest of her they tried to keep out. You've heard of stand-up comics? Her husband, Fang, can't stand her lying down.

Phyllis brags that she never made *Who's Who* but is featured in *What's That.*

Phyllis doesn't need anybody to put her down—nobody does it as well as she. "Most people get a reservation at a beauty ranch . . . I was committed." "When I go to a beauty parlor, I arrive by ambulance." "I'm looking for a perfume to overpower men—I'm sick of karate." "I made up my mind to show the world and they're afraid to look." "This dress hides the eighth wonder of the world."

Phyllis brags: "If I were a building, I'd be condemned." She says: "I wore a see-through dress—and nobody wanted to." Phyllis was dating a guy who was a body builder. She asked him what could he do for her body. He said, "Schedule it for demolition."

Phyllis told me, "I'm having a very bad week—my condo just went apartment."

Phyllis confides: "A peeping Tom called and told me to lower my shades."

BOB HOPE told her: "At least you're beautiful on the inside." She said "Leave it to me to be born inside out."

Some Phyllis killer dillers: "I had to give up exercising—I can't stand the noise." "Never refer to your wedding night as the original amateur hour."

There's even Phyllis Diller on philosophy: "Show me a man who doesn't turn around and gawk at a beautiful woman and I'll show you a man walking with his wife." "My advice to brides—burn the toast so he won't notice the coffee." Phyllis teaches: "Whatever you may look like, it's wise to marry a man your own age—as your beauty fades, so will his eye-sight."

Phyllis brags: "I make my biggest money renting myself out for Halloween parties."

I saw Phyllis Diller walk into a body parts shop, and before she could say a word, the manager looked her over and said, "Lady, if I were you I would junk it."

I asked Phyllis, "How do you keep your youth?" She said, "I lock him in the guest closet."

Phyllis Diller says young is better than old: "I asked this young man to run away with me. He said, '*You* go.' "

"Someone once asked my mother if everybody in our family suffered from insanity. She said, 'No, we all enjoyed it.' "

Phyllis lectures: "They aren't making mirrors the way they used to—the ones I buy now are full of wrinkles." "I had my face lifted, but it turned out there was one just like it underneath."

When the sexual revolution started a few years ago, Phyllis was on the casualty list: "A lot of my parts went AWOL. I nicknamed my water bed 'Lake Placid.' Our song was 'Taps.' "

Phyllis is proud to say: "I've turned many a head in my day—and a few stomachs, too." "I got a face lift—my face was sagging faster than the dollar."

RODNEY DANGERFIELD became a winner being a loser. "Lemme tell ya," Rodney told me, "it's not easy being me. I bought some rat poison—the girl said, 'Shall I wrap it up or are you gonna eat it here?' I called my doctor last week. I tell him, 'Doc. I swallowed a bottle of sleeping pills.' He told me to have a few drinks and get some rest."

As a kid, Rodney told his old man, "Nobody likes me." He said, "Don't say that—everybody hasn't met you yet." Even in the park he had no friends: "I'll never forget the see-saw—I had to keep running from one end to the other." "When I was a kid they bought me a carriage with no brakes. My first time at the beach, my old man gave the lifeguard five dollars to keep any eye *off* me."

Rodney was born with no respect: "One time I got lost. A cop helped me look for my parents. I said, 'Do you think we'll find them?' He said, 'I don't know, kid, there's so many places they could hide.' " As a grown-up, it was worse: "I told my date I'd like to see what her apartment looks like. She drew me a sketch." He met a girl at a dance and asked for her phone number. All she would give him was her area code.

He went on a blind date—and she turned out to be his wife. He's a guy with a dual personality—one worse than the other. He saved for years to buy an unbreakable, waterproof, shockproof, watch—and lost it.

Rodney told me, "My son goes to a private school—I've been trying for years to get him to tell me where it is."

Dangerfield made it fashionable to be a loser. For a guy who gets no respect, he made a fortune. Says Rodney, "I don't get no respect. I suspected my marriage was in trouble the first day—her parents sent me a thank you note."

Rodney explained the time he got no respect on a blind date: "I waited on the corner until this girl Louise walked by. I said, 'Are you Louise?' She said, 'Are you Rodney?' I said, 'Yes,' and she said, 'I'm not Louise.' " Rodney says he's always been unlucky in love: "My wife wants her sex in the back seat of a car—but she wants me to drive."

Rodney gets no respect anyplace: "My bank demands identification—even when I deposit money. I walked into a bank the other day. They had a sign that said, 'Deal with a bank you can trust—trust is everything'—and then I noticed that all of their pens are chained down. I got no luck at all. Last week I went in to buy a suit—my cash bounced.

I got no respect even as a kid—they played hide-and-seek and nobody would come look for me. I was in group therapy one time; they made me captain of the Paranoid Softball Team, but whenever I stole second base I'd feel guilty and go back."

Rod says: "I just don't get no respect. Every time I get in an elevator the operator says the same thing: 'Basement?' The superintendent in my building tells me to wipe my feet in my apartment before I go out in the hall. I brought a pet parrot home and it told me to get out."

"My kid came home depressed—he said he learned a new saying: 'Like father, like son.' The other night at dinner I said, 'Finish all your meat and you'll grow up just like Daddy—now he only eats vegetables. I took him to Coney Island and asked if he wanted to go in the crazy house—he told me to save my money, we'd be home soon. Another time my old man took me to a sideshow to see the freaks. The owner looked at me and said: 'Get the kid out of here, he's distracting from the show.' "

"Hey, I know I'm getting fat; are you kidding? I was so heavy, when I got my shoes shined I had to take the guy's word for it."

Rodney confided: "When I proposed I told my girl, 'Marry

me and I'll go to the ends of the earth for you.' After the wedding she said, 'OK, now you keep your end of the bargain.' "

Rodney told me: "Yes, I was once a tree surgeon, but so clumsy, I kept falling out of my patients!' Rodney claims: "Your whole life turns around when you hit middle age. You start to eat and you feel sexy—you go to bed and you feel hungry. By the time a man is able to read a woman like a book, his eyes go bad."

"No wonder I got no confidence in my looks—on Halloween, my parents sent me out as is. Even in my dreams I didn't get no respect. Once I dreamed I was kidnapped. The ransom note said, 'Pay us $5,000—or you'll see your kid again.' "

"When I was born, my father gave out cigar butts."

WOODY ALLEN: "My wife was an immature woman. I'd be in the bathroom taking a bath and she would walk right in and sink my boats. I spent thousands of dollars looking up my genealogy, and ten times that amount to keep it quiet. I'm going to my psychoanalyst one more year—then I'm going to Lourdes."

Woody is a winner who sounds like a loser and looks it: "I went to a psychoanalyst for years and it helped—now I get rejected by a much better class of girls. My parents didn't want me—they put a live teddy bear in my crib. I was kidnapped when I was a kid. Soon as my father got the ransom note, he sprang into action—he rented out my room."

JOEY BISHOP built himself up by putting himself down: "How did I hurt my back? I fell off a series. The series was canceled in spite of excellent ratings—one week we beat out *Let Us Pray.*" "I went to a computer dating service—and they sent me the number of Dial-a-Prayer." "When I performed in

Washington for the President, I didn't stay at the White
House—my mother wasn't crazy about the neighborhood."
"My wife just got her black belt in shopping." "My son has
had a steady job since he got out of college—he makes picket
signs for JANE FONDA."

JACK CARTER says, "I really know how to break up a party—
I join it." My friend Jack feels as forlorn and neglected as
Whistler's father. It all happened when he bought this beautiful little home in California: While digging in his back yard
last week he struck oil, and the gas station next door made
him pay for the repairs on their pipes.

Jack always carries a little card in his wallet that says,
"I'm a pessimist—in case of an accident, I'm not surprised."

JAN MURRAY said it: "You know it's going to be a bad day
if you wake up with your water bed busted—and you know
you ain't got a water bed."

NORM CROSBY: "I'm not illiterate—my parents were married." "I married kind of late in life. That's because when I
was younger I just couldn't find a girl who liked to do the
same things I liked to do. I liked to hang around the pool
room, drink beer, and chase girls—and I couldn't find a girl
who would do all of those things with me."

Norm philosophizes: 'Have you ever stopped to think that
when you go to court and face a jury you're putting your fate
into the hands of twelve men and women who weren't smart
enough to get out of jury duty?" "I asked my postman how
come it now takes three days for a letter from Los Angeles
to San Francisco, when the Pony Express used to deliver it in
two days. He told me it's because the horses got older and
can't run as fast now." "A friend of mine had a harrowing
experience. He locked his car with the keys in the ignition.
He stood there for two hours with a wire coat hanger, trying

unsuccessfully to fish the keys out through a narrow opening in the window. It was awful. His wife sat inside the car crying her heart out."

PAT COOPER: "My wife broke our dog of begging from the table—she let him taste it." Pat cries: "You don't have to tell me what my clothes look like—every year Goodwill gives me $500 *not* to clean out my closets. I've got to start dressing better—do you know how embarrassing it is to have people drop coins in your coffee cup?" "Would you believe that two magazines want *me* for the centerfold? *Field and Stream* and *Popular Mechanics*."

Self put-downs are the finest forms of flattening:

RIP TAYLOR: "My dentist called—he said my wisdom tooth is retarded." "My twin brother forgot my birthday." "I used to be married, but not anymore—now I send out." "My wife and I made love on a water bed—her side froze." "My wife was so frigid that when she opened her mouth, a light would come on." "I went to the Virgin Islands—they gave me a hero's welcome."

DOLLY PARTON said it herself: "I'm getting tired of carrying these things around—someday I'm going to let the air out." "You miss a lot by being built like me—onstage you can't see what's doing in the first six rows."

LUCILLE BALL said it: "I have everything I had twenty years ago—only it's all a little bit lower."

JOAN RIVERS hits pretty hard for a size four: "In school I had acne so bad my dog called me Spot." "I knew I was an unwanted baby when I saw that my bath toys were a toaster and a radio." "I got my start in show business modeling bras for Barbi dolls." "I was what you could call a war baby—my parents took one look at me and started fighting."

Joan preaches: "On the subject of birth control, my husband Edgar and I believe the simpler the better. Our idea of birth control is to just turn the lights on." "I once applied for a job as a topless waitress and wound up working as a busboy."

Joan was recounting her first love: "My first crush was a boy named Salvador Granford who lived down the block from me. I used to walk my dog back and forth in front of his house so many times his tree died."

Joan says: "My woes began when I went to a plastic surgeon for a face lift and I came home with PHYLLIS DILLER's old one."

Joan said she got an obscene phone call from her husband, telling her to clean the house.

Joan hollers: "What's the big deal about BO DEREK? I have the same measurements. Her living room is eighteen by twenty-five—and so is mine." "I'm crazy about FRANK SINATRA, but we're in litigation. I'm suing him for support for the four years I would have lived with him if he'd asked me." "I met WARREN BEATTY at a party. He said to me, 'You're *not* next.' "

Joan is the mouth that roars—even if it's against herself: "I was in a beauty contest once. I not only came in last—I was hit in the mouth by Miss Congeniality."

MILTON BERLE loves to roast himself: "I didn't have a great delivery when I was born, no matter what my mother told everybody." "I lost my TV show—I knew I was in trouble when I found 50 percent of the *studio* audience wasn't listening." "Did you notice the sign in front of the theater saying

'Welcome Milton Berle—The World's Greatest Comedian'? It really embarrassed me—they caught me putting up the sign."

Milton has a great philosophy: "If you live, there's nothing to worry about. If you don't live, you've only two things to worry about. Either you're going to heaven or you're not going to heaven. If you go to heaven, there's nothing to worry about, and if you go to the other place, you'll be so damn busy shaking hands with all your old friends, you won't have time to worry."

Even when he was in the hospital recently, he used jokes for a Band-Aid: "I was in the expensive-care unit." Milton moaned: "A laugh a day keeps the doctor away. So does not paying your bills." "I've got so many aches and pains that if a new one comes today, it will be at least two weeks before I can worry about it." Uncle Miltie says, "The only difference between an itch and an allergy is the size of the doctor's bill."

Every star builds himself up by putting himself down:

DEAN MARTIN: "If it weren't for pretzels and peanuts, I'd be on a liquid diet." "On champagne flights, some stewardesses serve too much. Once I got on as a passenger and got off as luggage."

Dean says he has come up with the perfect cure for a stiff neck: "Rub it with alcohol—from the *inside.*"

GEORGE BURNS says, "I'm at the age where sex is a four-letter word—*H-e-l-p.*" George Burns brags about his romantic prowess: "I'm a country singer—why shouldn't I be a country singer? I'm older than most countries. But I like to give advice to young lovers—I've got a good memory." One man wrote to George and asked about his sex life: "How can you do what you do at your age?" George answered, "I wear gloves." George says, "My sex life at ninety is just as great as it was when I was eighty-nine."

George Burns can't get old: "Of course I'm going to live to be one hundred—on my birthday, January 20, 1996, I start an engagement at the London Palladium for four weeks. I can't die—I'm booked." George's secret of youth? "I like to take young girls out to dinner—I hope some of their youth will rub off on me—and vice versa."

George Burns and BOB HOPE were sitting around the Friars watching to see whose foot would fall asleep faster. "What would you like people to be saying about you in a hundred years?" Bob asked. George answered, "That's easy—I'd like them to say, 'He looks good for his age.' " Bob said, "George, you look like a million—and we all know you couldn't be that old."

George Burns says, "I'm at the age where a miracle cure is anything that's paid for by Medicare." George preaches: "Retirement at sixty-five is ridiculous. When I was sixty-five I still had pimples." Now he's written a book, *Dr. Burns' Prescription for Happiness*, to prove his theory: "Happiness is a good martini, a good cigar and a good woman (or a bad woman, depending on just how much happiness you can take)."

George says: "My diet is simple: I eat anything that makes a noise in my mouth—bacon, carrot sticks, or French-fried potatoes. If it makes a noise, I feel like there's applause, and as I eat I can take bows." "Sex should be done behind locked doors. If what you're doing can be done in the open, you might as well be pitching horseshoes."

Throughout his career, George Burns has won over audiences with his generous spirit and sly wit; there are no signs

ROAST
of the
TOWN

that he intends to let up on us now. When asked what kind of epitaph he would prefer, his response is reassuring: "I don't care just as long as I'm around to read it."

A Handbook for
Politicians

The greatest weapon a politician can use is laughter, whether he's attacking or defending.

A long time ago RICHARD NIXON lost an election because of posters that read: "Would you buy a used car from this man?" Several elections before, THOMAS E. DEWEY blew it when he was sliced with "He looks like the groom on top of the wedding cake."

Nobody used gags to shoot down his opponents better than JOHN F. KENNEDY: "If Nixon runs unopposed he'll lose." Kennedy used his scalpel on everyone: "I like the straightforward way Senator McCARTHY dodges all those issues" and "BARRY GOLDWATER says he's standing on his record—that's so nobody can see it."

Another time he was accused of having had his father buy him the presidency. He solved this one with another laugh. At a White House correspondents' dinner, Kennedy read a telegram I gave him: "It's from my very generous daddy. It says, 'Dear Son, I don't mind paying for your election, but I refuse to pay for a landslide.' " The laughs drowned out the problem, and it never came up again. Kennedy laughed loudest when I said at one fund raiser for him, "Why are you worried about winning? If you lose the U.S., you can always buy Europe."

Of course, the President had the last word. He said to me, "I don't know what I'd do without you, but I'm willing to try."

I'm proud to be Irish. It was Saint Patrick who chased the snakes out of Ireland—now if only he'd do it in Washington.

RONALD REAGAN does it all with laughs: "The first time I ran for President I had to read for the part."

When JOHN ANDERSON said in one debate, "I'd rather be right than President," Ron said, "Don't worry—you'll never be either."

When JIMMY CARTER said, "Ronald Reagan is so far right he's on a bias," R.R. answered, "That's why Nancy likes to dance with me—I keep circling to to the right."

When some people complained that Reagan was for the rich, he laughed back, "What's wrong with rich? Listen, I've been rich and I've been poor, and believe me, rich is better. Sure a lot of people got money to burn. Why not? It's cheaper than gas."

I told the President I had some great political jokes for him. He said, "I don't need them—I appointed plenty on my own."

At one dinner I announced, "I found a sure way for Reagan to stay in Washington. He lets it drop that he plans to make a movie after he leaves the White House, whereupon the

American people will immediately pass a resolution making him President for life."

As Ronald Reagan says, "If we learn by our mistakes, we should have the best government on earth."

NELSON ROCKEFELLER had the greatest sense of humor of them all. He loved it when I picked on him. In fact, he insisted on it. He screamed the loudest when I said, "He's a self-made man. His father had billions but he treated Nelson like any normal kid. For Christmas he gave him a set of blocks—Fiftieth Street, Fifty-first Street, Fifty-second Street . . ."

At one big dinner at the Rainbow Room, Rockefeller asked me to be the toastmaster: "We will have the President, the cardinal, a couple of dozen senators, Governor Reagan, Nixon, Agnew, and all the moneymen in town; it's got to be the dullest gathering of the year. So I want you to go to work on them. Roast them all, leave nobody out, and start with me." Who am I to argue with the governor of my state?

When Rockefeller introduced me, he said, "OK, Joey Adams, you're a comedian, tell us a joke." I said, "OK, Nelson Rockefeller, you're a politician, tell us a lie." The governor laughed the loudest, and we were off.

The first celebrity I introduced was TERENCE CARDINAL COOKE. "I better not make any jokes about his Eminence," I said. "The last time I did it, it snowed in my living room for three weeks."

I said to SPIRO AGNEW, "Your ability and sincerity have never been questioned, or even mentioned, come to think of it."

I introduced RICHARD NIXON as the greatest President:

"That's not only my opinion, it's his, too . . . Mr. Nixon is beginning to make noises like he'd like to run again. I suggest the border."

HENRY KISSINGER was next on my list: "Kissinger is a very religious man. He worships himself. I hear he's changing his faith—he no longer believes he's God. The only problem with Henry is, when you enter his office you have to kiss his ring. I wouldn't mind, only he keeps it in his back pocket."

The laughs were coming fast and furious. "Now," I said, "the governor wants me to treat everybody equally. If I can pick on his Eminence, I can pick on anybody. After all, I have a right. I did a Catholic benefit last night. I know it was a Catholic benefit because I left my car in front of the hotel and they raffled it off.

"Now, let's take care of the Polish situation . . ." One man, in full dress, stood up in the center of the ballroom and shouted, "Before you go any further, Mr. Adams, I think you ought to know that I am Polish." A hush came over the room. All the laughs were nothing now, and the President, the governor, the entire audience sat there stunned. I said to the man, "I beg your pardon, what did you say?" He said again, louder, "I want you to know that *I am Polish*." I said, "That's OK. I'll speak slower." The audience screamed, the President banged the table, and Rockefeller threw his glass in the air. The crisis was over, and a laugh was the cure again.

If you're going to run for office, I'm going to prepare you for everything but failure. A politician should keep his words soft, honeyed, and warm. He never knows when he might be called upon to eat them, so the funnier the better.

A good laugh can get you out of any problem. When my good friend Nelson Rockefeller was running for governor, his opponent was ARTHUR GOLDBERG. I thought it would be a good idea if Nelson went to the Borscht Belt with me, ate cheese blintzes, danced with the Jewish ladies, and even stuffed himself with bagels, cream cheese, and lox.

He was a hit until the next day, when Arthur Goldberg called a press conference and said, "Rockefeller was compromising the Jews." It was a blow to my friend, who loved everyone. "What will I say?" he asked me. I said, "Let me answer when you hold the next press conference."

The first question was "Did you hear Arthur Goldberg say you were compromising the Jews? Well?" Rocky said, "My pal Joey will answer that one." I said, "Goldberg is a nice Jewish man. My Uncle Morris is also a nice Jewish man. My uncle shouldn't be governor, and neither should Goldberg." The laughs drowned out his whole complaint. I added, "Goldberg is the dullest speaker in the country. If he makes one more speech, Rockefeller will carry Canada."

LYNDON JOHNSON was another President who cloaked his political hide with a covering of wit. When Johnson decided against seeking another term, thus becoming a hero overnight, he commented ruefully, "Sure, everybody loves his mother-in-law when she's leaving."

In his personal life, Johnson's humor expanded to accommodate his ego. One day he invited a group of pals to a barbecue on his ranch. Like all Texans, he was bragging: "I've got three thousand head of cattle here." His neighbor interrupted, "Mr. President, I don't want to bring you down, but every rancher in Texas has at least three thousand head of cattle." The President cracked, "In his refrigerator?"

L.B.J. had hundreds of phone numbers at the ready, and he often dialed personally because he wanted fast answers. Being preoccupied with lesser matters, such as the state of the Union, he wasn't clued into the fact that I had gotten into show business so I could sleep late. "Mr. Adams, please," said President Johnson pleasantly when he called me one 11:00 A.M.

"He's asleep," answered my new Estonian housekeeper, whose first day on the job had come with instructions that I was not to be awakened before noon. Not by anybody. Not even the President of the United States.

L.B.J. insisted. "This is the White House. It's important that I speak to Mr. Adams."

She answered: "Look, buster, I don't care what color is your house. I told you he's sleeping and I don't wake him for nobody. I wouldn't wake him for the President of the United States."

Johnson's voice rose. "This *is* the President."

"So call back," she snapped, and hung up.

Thirty minutes later I received the message that "Some president from a white house called." When I telephoned President Johnson, he uttered but one comment: "If there's ever a price on your head—take it."

When I was a kid, I knew that all fairy tales began with the line "Once upon a time." Now that I'm grown up, I know that all fairy tales begin with the line "If I'm elected . . ."

To be elected and live happily ever after today, the Good Fairy had better have funny tales. Heavy-handed pols are learning that they need a good-humor man in the budget. It is for this reason that I have written this handbook of wit for politicians. Listen, if Nixon had saved up jokes instead of tapes, he'd be a television star today.

They tell me now that NIXON was as sexy as KENNEDY. I just can't believe it. If Nixon had an affair in office, I misjudged him. I thought he was just doing it to the country.

Recently I was asked to roast a group of stars who were in the lineup at a conservative-party dinner at the Sheraton Center. "This dais looks like a meeting of the fan club of Attila the Hun," I started. Honor guest V.P. GEORGE BUSH, WILLIAM BUCKLEY, JACK KEMP, AL D'AMATO, and HENRY KISSINGER laughed the loudest—they had no choice:

"It is said that Jack Kemp is the next President of the United States, and tonight we honor the man who said it—Jack Kemp."

"There is only one Alfonse D'amato—I found that out by looking it up in the telephone directory.

"I want to say to William Buckley—you are the most didactic, ubiquitous, and pristine, if not eleemosynary, personality of our times—and I say that without fear of contradiction—and without knowing what I'm talking about. I'll use words, Bill, you put them where you think they belong.

"I was talking to Henry Kissinger—through one of his interpreters. Henry has been in this country forty years—and he sounds like he's arriving next Thursday."

RONALD REAGAN said, "Kissinger is a man who had greatness thrust upon him—and ducked."

Henry answered, "Reagan reminds me of JOE NAMATH—boy, can he throw it."

I've got a better one for you, Henry: "Reagan has done the work of two men—LAUREL AND HARDY."

I supply the gags to all sides. May the one who gets the biggest laughs win: "Reagan is so conservative he wants to change the Republican party symbol from an elephant to a dinosaur. He promises if he's reelected, he will legalize snuff."

I got Ronnie's answer: "If the Democrats get elected, it could be the dawn of a new error."

HENRY KISSINGER called Reagan a unique statesman. And everybody knows what a statesman is. That's a politician who never got caught.

Vice-President George Bush says, "The trouble with our foreign relations is that they're all broke."

R.R. said, "I made so much money betting on the Democrats that I became a Republican."

The Democrats are loaded with ammunition, too: "Reagan wants to run again, and he'll probably be elected. Sure, they always return to the scene of the crime."

Reagan always has the last laugh: "I haven't seen that much teamwork among the Democratic party in Washington since Congress voted itself a raise."

As I was saying at the conservative-party dinner: "Politics is such a precarious business—as I was telling my waiter here, WALTER MONDALE."

Congress voted itself a raise. They had to because since ABSCAM, the FBI cut out giving bribes. It's not nice to call people liars—that's why we call them congressmen. The Congress says it wants to raise our hopes for a better life. For a better life I don't need my hopes raised. I need my taxes lowered.

More and more congressmen now stay in Washington all year round because they can't live at home under the laws they've passed. There's still a double standard—the place where a woman sells herself is called a house of ill repute; the place where a man sells himself is called the House of Representatives.

Reagan explains his policy: "Charity begins at home, but why does it have to wind up in every foreign country?"

GEORGE BUSH says, "The trouble with foreign aid is, it allows too many nations to live beyond our means."

I got the jokes and the gags to get them all in and out of trouble and in and out of office—which is the same thing. I'm not taking sides. All I can say is, may the best man win. The trouble is, he's not running this year.

The whole world congratulated Ronald Reagan on his seventy-fifth birthday, February 6. He is now more popular than ever. I'm very proud of him—if he was still an actor, he'd be too old to *play* President. FREDDIE ROMAN notes, "He looks just great for a seventy-five-year-old man with nine-year-old hair." It's amazing how he's improved with age—today he's a much better actor.

It was a great day for the Prez—the heat from his birthday cake melted all the jelly beans in the jar on his desk. NANCY REAGAN wanted to surprise him by digging up some of the old pals who grew up with him—and she'd have to—like MARY MILES MINTER, GYPSY ROSE LEE, W. C. FIELDS, and the ever popular MAE BUSH. She even tried to get the band that played at his prom—JOHN PHILIP SOUSA. She felt bad that his buddies who signed the Declaration of Independence couldn't join him for his birthday.

Let's not forget this is America, where any kid can grow

up to be President—if he becomes a movie star first. I saw a Ronald Reagan movie on TV, and I'm convinced we were right in electing him—think how awful it would be if he continued making movies. Reagan is still waiting for a pardon from the Chief Justice for *Bedtime for Bonzo*." His big trouble is his advisers: CURLY, LARRY, AND MOE.

I am strictly for his policies: Talk tough and carry a big bag of jelly beans. Also, he's promised to deal very harshly with terrorist organizations—I mean, it's about time somebody took a strong stand against the I.R.S.

For his birthday, we recall some historic Reagan lines: "Scientists will soon come up with a perfect political vaccine for foot-in-the-mouth disease." "Government machinery is the marvelous device which enables ten men to do the work of one." Advice to politicos: Always be sincere, whether you mean it or not. Ron's sense of humor is the greatest: "My esteem in the country has gone up—now when people wave at me, they use all five fingers."

The Prez says, "It's too bad that all the people who know how to run the country are busy driving taxis or cutting hair. One citizen wrote me, 'Why should we send advisers to the Middle East—if we've got people who give good advice, let's send them to Washington.' "

Ronald Reagan has the greatest sense of humor of any President in history. I didn't know George Washington too well, and I didn't exactly pal around with Grover Cleveland, but I do know Reagan—he can throw a punch line better than any stand-up comic. After his shooting, he told us all, "If I'd gotten this much attention in Hollywood, I never would have left." When he opened his eyes after the operation, he said to Nancy and waiting world, "I'm sorry, honey, I forgot to duck."

Ronald's opening line at one dinner: "Holding office, especially the presidency, is like trying to dance at a disco—no matter what you do, you've got to rub somebody the wrong way." One reporter asked, "You've been around in politics a long time and you sure must have seen some mighty big changes, right, Mr. President?" Reagan said, "I sure have—and I've been against them all."

Reagan said, "We got another problem—teaching the Marine Band to play the minuet."

We all know we can do any jokes about the Prez without any kickback. BOB HOPE said: "There has been another switch in the White House. Nancy and Ronald Reagan have changed jobs, and now *he* will run the country for a while." I said: "Reagan is a modern politician—he claims he was born in a log condo."

MILTON BERLE: "Nancy wore clothes from four designers for the inaugural gala—and wouldn't you know it, BOY GEORGE showed up wearing the same thing."

I said, "Reagan's economic theory is simple: We have a deficit because the poor people are hoarding all the money."

MICHAEL REAGAN is taking acting lessons for an upcoming TV role. When asked if he wanted to become a good actor, he said, "No, I want to follow in my father's footsteps."

Reagan wrote this poem to MONDALE: "Your wit and wisdom I've often enjoyed, Sorry I had to make you unemployed."

Listen, I'm for Reagan all the way. When he says something, people know he's not lying—he was never that good an actor.

The Prez loves to roast himself. During the election he

pointed out that the Roman emperor Diocletian had tried price controls and they hadn't worked. Then Reagan added, "And I'm the only one here old enough to remember that."

He also loves to roast others. When TIP O'NEILL lumbered into his office and took up two seats, the Prez remarked, "It looks like my policies are the only things that Tip can't swallow."

But the President is carrying his cowboy image a little too far—when he signs legislation, he uses a branding iron.

I still don't know if it was a blooper when the President said, "For some reason, I sleep better when Congress is in recess." Our man in the White House asks: "Have you read the *Congressional Record*? It's almost like a religious experience: It passeth all understanding." Sez I: I won't say what it's accomplished, but this could be the first Congress ever arrested for loitering.

President Reagan has done a lot for women. By not naming many to high government posts, he's giving them the opportunity of seeking better-paying jobs in private industry. The Prez says, "What do you mean I don't treat women as equals? Didn't I appoint a woman to the Supreme Court? Of course, she isn't paid as much as the guys."

I love Ronald Reagan. Right after the assassination attempt, he endeared himself to all. In the operating room, he looked up at the attending surgeons and said, "I hope you're all Republicans."

He uses his wit as a weapon and his wisdom as a pacifier. "It's a good thing that Moses didn't have to submit The Ten Commandments to Congress for approval." At one press conference he noted: "Some members of Congress ought to have their mouths taped instead of their speeches." The President

Ed Sullivan was such a colossal stone face, with no significant personality, that roasting him was hard work *(Friars Club)*.

Mitch Miller and Johnny what's-his-name.

George Burns could roast Jack Benny just by saying hello. Two pros.

Top: *New York's former Mayor Beame and Governor Carey applaud Frank and Frank Junior at the Sinatra roast* **(Friars Club).**

Middle: *One of the Friars' first dinners. George M. Cohan, Enrico Caruso, Victor Herbert, Will Rogers, Irving Berlin, and a few hundred other American ultras* **(Friars Club).**

Right: *Mickey Rooney always looked up to me. He had to.*

Left: *Ron did a lot for show business—he left it.* Right: *Georgie Jessel's wit, timing, and delivery made him one of the most sought-after toastmasters. Also, he worked cheap* **(Whitestone Photo).** Bottom: *"Is that a dimple on your chin, Bob, or the place they inflate your head?"*

Top: *"Dial-a-prayer is holding all calls until after the dinner, Frank."*
Middle: *Buddy Hackett smiles and Johnny Carson waits for the next zinger at the Carson roast.*
Bottom: *Dinah Shore was one of the first Roastettes. Here with George Montgomery, as Phil Silvers introduces Burt Reynolds* **(Friars Club)**.

Berle, Jan Murray, Red
Buttons, and a glass of
Geritol **(Friars Club).**

Cindy, Dolly Parton,
Dolly Parton, and myself.

Just another pretty face,
along with Alan King and
Phyllis Diller.

Left: *Jerry Lewis is famous for his humility. Believe me, he has a lot to be humble about* **(Friars Club)**. Right: *Breaking up Buckley. Who would have thought he knew any four-letter words?* Bottom: *Cosell and Robert Merrill put the squeeze on Dick Cavett. Love your hair, Howard* **(Friars Club)**.

Left: *Liz Taylor handled the fat jokes with real class. She got thin.* **Right:** *Try that gag again, Mr. President. On second thought, maybe you should just show us your scar.* **Bottom:** *That special face.*

Top: *Don't laugh too soon, Frank, her mother is under the table* **(Friars Club)**. Middle: *Standing: Dean Martin, Joe E. Lewis, and Georgie Jessel. Dean Martin—standing?!* Bottom: *Cary Grant wondering how he got into this mess, as his wife, Barbara, wonders how he'll get out of it.*

reminisces: "When I was a kid my father worked in a store; we lived above the store. It's no different from the White House, except now I go to work in an elevator." The wisdom comes when he has to leave the White House: "My German problems were caused by my own hearing impairment—I thought they wanted me in *Pittsburg*."

Reagan delivers one-liners as well as a stand-up comic: "He's a politician trying to save both his faces at once." "Imagine having two TIP O'NEILL's." "Washington is the only city where sound travels faster than light." "I can define middle age—it's when you're faced with two temptations, and you choose the one that'll get you home by nine o'clock." The last time I saw the President I said, "You look like a million." He said, "Oh, now you're talking about my age."

BOB HOPE and Ronald Reagan met on the golf course. "What's your handicap?" Bob asked. "The Congress," the President answered.

The President's wit hits everybody equally: "You remember Congress; it has two chambers—Sodom and Gomorrah."

At one press conference, R.R. said, "JESSE HELMS wants me to move to the right; LOWELL WEICKER wants me to move to the left; TEDDY KENNEDY wants me to move back to California." "People often ask what I intend to do for the sick, the senile and elderly. Well, that's easy. I plan to introduce legislation to see that members of Congress serve only one term."

Ronnie said, "I do *not* dye my hair—I'm just prematurely orange."

Even the President has to file an income tax report. "Tell me Mr. President, do you have any liabilities?" "Well, take my cabinet—please."

The Prez says, "Politics is like kissing—you don't have to be good at it to enjoy it."

Ronald Reagan said it: "It's always easy to tell a successful executive. He's the one who can delegate all the responsibility, shift all the blame, and appropriate all the credit."

The President's favorite story: The American said, "Look, in my country I can walk into the Oval Office; I can hit the desk with my fist and say, 'President Reagan, I don't like the way you're governing the United States.' And the Russian said, 'I can do that.' The American said, 'What?' He said, 'I can walk into the Kremlin, hit GORBACHEV's desk, and I can say, 'Mr. President, I don't like the way Ronald Reagan is governing the United States.'"

Here are some great wild lines you can use on the right politician at the right time:

You could use many words to describe him. You could say humble, you could say modest, you could say unassuming. You'd be wrong—but you could say them.

He has more talent in his little finger than he has in his big finger.

He's quite a man. You can talk to him on any subject. He doesn't understand—but you can talk to him.

As far as I'm concerned, the only reason we have elections is to find out if the polls are right. A new poll released this month shows that 85 percent of the Americans polled are completely confused about U.S. foreign policy. Now, that's a pretty alarming figure—especially when you consider that the poll was taken at the State Department.

It's Election Day. Squirrels will be gathering nuts—and we'll be voting for them. Make sure you vote for the best man—whether he's running or not. And don't be taken in by silver-tongued orator's cheap rhetoric, phony promises, political claptrap, patriotic publicity, slick commercials, and campaign jazz—just flip a coin.

It was **RONALD REAGAN** who said, "If you go to the polls and elect me, your troubles may not be over—but mine will." **MONDALE**'s bid for the presidency was best summed up in the work of Benjamin Franklin: Better he should go fly a kite.

Did you hear about the Ronald Reagan bra? Supports the right and ignores the left.

Mondale says he's going to stand on his record—but he won't be able to stand on anything until he gets his foot out of his mouth.

I listened to all the debates and I still can't understand it. When I make up stories they call them jokes—when politicians make up stories they call them campaign promises.

Talking too much can cause headaches—every time **TIP O'NEILL** opens his mouth, Reagan gets a headache.

Tip keeps saying too many people in the country have nothing to eat—and he looks like the one who's been getting their share.

Let's hope the Prez gets us out of debt by the time he leaves office—how will it look if Reagan has to ride off into the sunset on a borrowed horse?

Ronald Reagan has been saying some very funny things lately. There are some who say he should be in show business—but who listens to TIP O'NEILL.

I've listened to guys in Congress explain their plan to solve the country's problems, and let me tell you, the guys on Mount Rushmore aren't the only politicians with rocks in their heads.

Reagan may throw a lot of jokes but I happen to agree with his way of handling people. I think he is right to start talks with the very people who pose the biggest threat to our nation and who could cause us the most harm—the Russians and Congress.

All we need to solve all our problems is some horse sense. The president has the horse—now let's put some sense in the Senate.

Here are some political one-liners—use them at your own discretion:

There are two sides to every question—and a good politician takes both.

A politician is the fellow who is always ready to lay down *your* life for *his* country.

You rarely see a thin politician. It's because of all those words they have to eat.

Most politicians suffer from the same problem—too much bone in the head and not enough in the back.

A good politician knows how to say nothing. He just doesn't always know when. He can talk for an hour without mentioning what he was talking about.

The trouble with most of today's politicians is that they try to show us they're part of the common herd by throwing us a lot of bull.

The secret of politicians is, never open your mouth unless you have nothing to say.

Give a politician enough rope and he'll hang you.

My neighbor says he hates busing: "My daughter was forced to go to school with a minority group—Democrats."

In a recent poll, 42 percent of the voters approved of the job Reagan is doing, 30 percent were not happy, and 28 percent tried to borrow money from the guy taking the poll.

Politics is not a bad profession. If you succeed, there are many rewards. If you disgrace yourself or go to jail, you can always write a book.

Politicians are divided into three groups: the anointed, the appointed, and the disappointed.

In crime, the theory is take the money and run. In politics, it's run—then take the money.

Politicians are sworn to take it—"I'm not really as good as you said, but I'm much better than you're thinking." At one dinner for Senator D'AMATO I started, "I've known some of the best politicians money could buy—not you, Senator." The double laugh satisfied the people and the senator. At a function for Congressman MARIO BIAGGI I noted, "The disadvantage of giving a politician a free hand is he usually winds up putting it in your pocket—not you, Mario." Nobody laughed harder than Biaggi.

At one dinner I said: "I think MONDALE is the man to get this country moving again. I know if he came into my neighborhood, *I'd* move."

"Some people think our Presidents should be limited to a single six-year term. Personally, I think all politicians should be given six-year terms—with possible time off for good behavior."

One girl said to another, "What I'm looking for is a man who will treat me as if I were a voter and he was a candidate."

It's useless to try to hold a person to anything he says while he's in love, drunk, or running for office.

Politics is a game of give-and-take, with more takers than givers.

Politics is the art of obtaining money from the rich and votes from the poor, on the pretext of protecting each from the other.

There's a bill now that will solve this latest problem. If passed, it will make all bribes to public officials taxable.

What would happen if everybody believed what political candidates say about each other and nobody won?

You can laugh a politician into or out of office. The politician is the easiest target. He approaches every subject with an open mouth. Every politician says he talks straight from the shoulder—too bad his words don't start from higher up. Lis-

ten, if half the statements of opposing politicians are true, none of these guys are fit to hold public office.

I had so little trust in my congressman that when he admitted he lied, I didn't believe him.

It's silly for the Russians to accuse us of spying to find out what's going on in Moscow. We're kept too busy trying to find out what's going on in Washington.

The President loves those European trips. He just loves visiting countries that are younger than he is.

I get nervous when Congress is in session—these guys can do more damage than Rambo.

The Republicans are putting out a handy *Guide to Politics: Knowing Your Ass from Your Elephant*.

According to recent studies, the best cure for insomnia is now believed to be a civil service job.

NANCY REAGAN keeps asking: "What do you wear to a recession?"

There is no truth to the rumor that if someone in the White House tells a lie, NIXON gets a residual.

The President says business is good—but then, he's got a better location and he doesn't have to pay rent.

RONALD REAGAN is still the hero of the average man—the Dow Jones industrial average man.

When they call a candidate a favorite son these days, that's the greatest unfinished sentence in history.

He couldn't see a belt without hitting below it.

If you believe what the candidates are saying about each other, it would be impossible to vote for anyone.

This is the land of promise—especially before Election Day.

Did you ever notice how when somebody you know personally is nominated for office you are torn between local pride and fear for the country?

Any man who points an accusing finger should remember that he has three fingers pointing at himself.

A politician had a secret popularity poll taken—now he wants to make sure it's kept that way.

There are too many candidates running this year. There may not be enough campaign promises to go around.

Take a look at our taxes and you'll stop calling them cheap politicians.

He speaks his mind—the only trouble is that it limits his conversation.

_____ is my second choice for office—my first choice is anybody who runs against him.

When J.F.K. was President, BOBBY KENNEDY had no sense of humor about himself. He insisted on being called Robert. When J.F.K. passed on, Robert became Bobby and he decided he was now big enough to take it—and like it. I became his favorite roastmaster because, as he put it, I was his equalizer.

At one fall-guy luncheon I hit him with everything, and he loved it.

"Robert Kennedy has a vigorous image—he has ten children. Everybody thinks that's because he's a devout Catholic. Not so—he's a sex maniac.

"When he come home he doesn't ask, 'What's new?' He asks, 'Who's new?'

"George Washington may have been called the father of our country—but Bobby Kennedy *is*.

"When he married Ethel he promised her the world—and he damn near gave it to her.

"I just found out he is going to India to teach birth control. It was President JOHNSON's suggestion—he said, 'Let's give Bobby back to the Indians.'

"They call him a carpetbagger—they said he doesn't know New York and has no right to run for senator. All lies—so what if he thought Rockefeller Center was the governor's navel?

"I happen to know that Bobby Kennedy does not want to be President—he wants to be King.

"Everybody loves Bobby. Cardinal Cooke was going to be here today, but he didn't want to kiss Bobby's ring again."

PART II

The Friars Roasts

Jimmy Stewart

The Friars Roast of JIMMY STEWART brought out some great names and some great name-calling:

BURT REYNOLDS: "We're here tonight to honor Jimmy Stewart . . . a sex symbol for women who no longer care."

LUCILLE BALL: "Jimmy Stewart is sort of square. Even in the early days he told me that his idea of a romantic evening was soft light, sweet music, champagne . . . no girl—just soft light, sweet music, and champagne."

JESSE WHITE: "I did *Harvey* on the road with Jimmy Stewart, and even then Jimmy was easy going and people took advantage of him. One night Jimmy gave a bellhop a hundred-dollar bill and said, 'Bring me a couple of hamburgers and get something for yourself.' When the man came back with the food, Jimmy asked for his change and the bellhop said, 'You told me to get something for myself . . . I got a wristwatch.' I'll never forget how nice Jimmy was about it. He said to the bellhop, 'Would you mind if I call you once in a while and ask what time it is?' "

MICKEY ROONEY: There's a statue of James Stewart in the

Hollywood Wax Museum . . . and the statue talks faster than he does."

GLORIA STEWART: "What you've said about my husband is true. He is cautious and conservative. Who else wears suspenders and a belt . . . with his pajamas?"

Johnny Carson

Roastmaster **BOB HOPE** hit first: "We are saluting Johnny Carson, the patron saint of insomniacs.

"I have great respect for Johnny. It's not often I've met someone who's stolen more from NBC than I have.

"You've seen his show. He keeps asking, 'What do I hold up?' The last four times it's been NBC.

"I admire a man who can do what John has done to his network . . . as many times, as many ways, and as many positions.

"Johnny Carson has a terrific contract with NBC. If he dies they bury **RICH LITTLE**.

"How about Johnny's new deal with NBC, $2.5 million a year for twenty-five weeks, three days a week. He makes the Brinks mob look like the **PAT BOONE** family.

"All them NBC brass are here tonight, John. They're buttering your bread, filling your glass, cutting your steak, and kissing your ring.

"This man has had a fabulous career. I'm sure when he was a simple farmboy in Nebraska he never dreamed that one day he'd be the busiest John in America."

Looking at baby Johnny in a blanket, his mother said, "Those tiny arms, he'll never be a boxer. Those tiny legs, he'll never be a runner." And his father said, "He'll never be a porno film star, either."

Johnny's great. He gives older folks something to laugh about in bed.

RED BUTTONS was loving: "Carson has done as much for the Friars Club as panty hose has done for sex."

ALAN KING: "I hope you will all live as long as this evening has seemed to me."

MIKE WALLACE: "Johnny once introduced me on his show as the proctologist of the interview. We all know what anatomical item it is a proctologist deals with. Well, last Sunday on *Sixty Minutes* in interviewing Johnny Carson this proctologist dealt with the biggest one of all."

HOWARD K. SMITH (a man who has been bringing on the national news for so long I think his first broadcast described Moses crossing the Red Sea): "Johnny went into the men's room, followed by his agent. John pulled out his hankerchief and a dime fell out and into the toilet. The agent was horrified. He couldn't imagine a national figure having to reach into the toilet. Johnny was unperplexed. He reached into his pocket, pulled out a quarter, and threw it in. The agent said, 'What did you do that for?' Johnny said, 'Well, for ten cents I couldn't reach down there, but for thirty-five cents I may be able to make it.'"

BOB HOPE on LUCILLE BALL: "In four movies Lucy played

my wife and we did passionate love scenes. And at night she went home to her real husband. The story of my life. I gas up the car and someone else goes for the joyride."

LUCILLE BALL: "The Republican party offered to run Johnny Carson for the Senate. They want him to do what RONALD REAGAN did—get the hell out of show business."

"I like Johnny," I said lovingly. "One thing I can tell you— this new multi-million-dollar contract with NBC has not changed him. He's still the same arrogant bastard he always was."

JOHNNY CARSON: "Thank you for a wonderful evening. The show has run a little long. I should mention that when HELEN HAYES arrived here tonight she was jailbait."

On BOB HOPE: "As you know this is the seventy-fifth anniversary of the Friars, and coincidentally, seventy-five years ago the Friars had their first dinner, and the guest of honor was GEORGE M. COHAN. And, Bob, I understand you did a terrific job as MC that night, too.

"For those of you who are unfamiliar with the Friars, basically it is a multi-million-dollar fraternal organization that was founded in order to give GENE BAYLOS and HENNY YOUNG-MAN a place to steam.

"My good friend and a longtime friend of the *Tonight* show, DAVID TEBET, informed me that the Friars were establishing a seat in my honor, and I was quite thrilled until I saw it. I thought the least they could've done was to remove the paper strip that said 'Sanitized for your protection.' "

It was a great night: The Friars voted to have Johnny Carson's tongue bronzed while he was still alive.

Jerry Lewis

Now let's examine Jerry Lewis the man—and this man should have been examined years ago.

The Friars chose JOHNNY CARSON for the operation: "I've been roastmaster on four occasions to great comedians, and tonight it is for Jerry Lewis. This is known as the law of diminishing returns.

"During the evening there will be a lot of caustic remarks made at Jerry, but I'd like to point out that these are done with great affection—and if you buy that I also have some swampland in New Jersey I would like to unload.

"Jerry is a very unique individual—he is the only man that was belted in the mouth by Mahatma Ghandi."

Johnny was eloquent: "I would like to introduce RED SKELTON but I'm stuck with ALAN KING. He goes down to the slums where he was born many times to see a reminder of his youth—his mother and father."

ALAN KING: "Jerry has been described as a twentieth-century phenomenon—well, like the moon landings, nobody talks about that anymore; like atomic energy, it's the biggest bomb we ever had; and like a heart transplant, he is always being rejected."

I was glad to pay my disrespect: "Jerry Lewis is very hot in France these days—but you must remember that at one time so was Joan of Arc."

MILTON BERLE: "HENNY YOUNGMAN wants to be remembered by anybody . . . It is indeed an honor to be here tonight to praise this Jewish Huntz Hall, the only man to get a Dear John letter from Typhoid Mary. A lot of people fought over who was to be on this dais tonight, and those that won aren't here. Jerry came from a poor family—they had one room, so Jerry always slept with his mother and father and never knew what it was like to sleep alone until after he got married. Where else but here in this democratic country would you see an Italian kid like Dean and a Jewish kid like Jerry get together . . . and the Italian kid would have the nose job."

JACK CARTER: "Jerry has done more for my career in show business than anyone else. He made forty-three movies and kept me out of all of them. What a charitable man—last year the old age home came to him and he gave them a tremendous donation: his mother and father."

JERRY LEWIS: "Thank you very much to my pallbearers. On the dais tonight are really extraordinary people—and I'm going to get every one of them. I must say that to follow great comedy like this I would be a fool to try and top that. A lot of you might think I'm saying that because it's best to choose to go the other way. I wouldn't attempt to top them. I know I couldn't if I tried—and with that kind of humility I must get off to a big hand. In summing up, I'm honored to be here tonight—I didn't realize the spritzes would be like they were, but these are the people I have grown up with in the business.

They are beautiful people, and if you were to sit here you would feel the loving side of their ambivalence and be terribly proud to be the brunt of their humor. Thank you very much."

George Burns

It was George Burns's ninetieth birthday. A bunch of us were sitting at the Friars, trying to figure the best way to honor our oldest and most beloved Friar. "There's only one way," said JEAN-PIERRE TREBOT, our executive director, "we've got to roast him good—and make it well done. It's the only way to show our love."

"But," said IRWIN ROSEE, the editor of the Friars' *Epistle*, "He's ninety years old. Won't his family resent it?"

"Not on your life," said AL RYLANDER, our public relations director, "they'll think you don't love him if we don't put him down like we do to all our stars."

At the Friars, roasting is a way of life. They not only expect it, they demand it.

I walked into the club at lunchtime the other day and saw old pal HOWARD COSELL. "Glad to see you, Howard, where you been?" I greeted him. "What's the matter," he growled, "are you mad at me?" I said, "No, of course not—why do you ask?" He said, "Because you said 'hello' so nicely, without one louse-up." "Oh, I'm sorry," I apologized, "I never heard you say an unkind word about anybody. That's because you never talk about anybody but yourself. I hear you recently went out of your mind—and nobody knew." Howard said, "Now that's better—now I know you love me. By the way, you sure have a fertile mind—and you know what makes things fertile." I knew he loved me to.

See that's how we do it at the Friars.

MILTON BERLE said, "HENNY YOUNGMAN is king of the one-liners. That's because he can't remember two."

When SYLVESTER STALLONE got married recently, JOHNNY CARSON knifed, "How did the bride get him to tear him away from himself?"

DEAN MARTIN said, "MERV GRIFFIN is responsible for more television sets being sold than anybody else—I know I sold mine, my son sold his, and my neighbor sold his . . ."

What can you say about DON RICKLES that hasn't been said about poison ivy? Don says he only roasts the ones he loves. If that's true, he has had more lovers than an Eighth Avenue hooker.

See what I mean? How could we do less for our beloved George Burns?
A lot of his pals met at the Friars Club in New York and California to love the hell out of him. George warned all his comic pals: "I don't want any special treatment on my nineti-eth birthday—I want to be roasted like everybody else—and if you don't, I won't invite you to my hundredth birthday party."

WALTER MATTHAU said, "George Burns deserves the party.

He's a father figure to most girls—they keep asking him for money."

JACKIE GLEASON noted, "George reads *Playboy* for the same reason he reads *National Geographic*—to see places he'll never get to visit."

MILTON BERLE: "I have to say this about my friend George— he looks just the same today as he looked forty years ago— old."

JOHNNY CARSON: "George has been on my show twenty or thirty times, or maybe more. How can you turn down a guy that age?'

JACK CARTER: "There's one thing you can say about George, he wears well—but so do my army shoes."

RED BUTTONS: "George Burns, what a man. He read in the paper that it takes ten dollars a year to support a kid in India. So he sent his kids there."

BOB HOPE: "The first time I saw George Burns on the stage I could see he had what it took to become a big star—Gracie Allen."

JOAN RIVERS: "Since I met him ten years ago there hasn't been a day that I didn't think of George Burns. And I didn't think of him again today."

STEVE ALLEN: "I was very excited about George's last book, because I thought it was."

CAROL CHANNING: "George has been playing the part so long he really believes he's God—only older."

BOB HOPE interrupted to say, "George Burns, LAWRENCE

WELK and I, for excitement on Saturday night, sit around and see whose leg falls asleep faster—then we try to contact the living."

STEVE ALLEN: "George is a great comedian—he's been a star of stage, TV, nightclubs, pictures, for years. And I finally figured out the reason for his success—he's never improved."

JOEY BISHOP said, "What's old? Both Georges—Washington and Burns—got their teeth from the same carpenter."

FREDDIE ROMAN: "George Burns is at the age where his sex drive is in park."

DEAN MARTIN: "The hardest thing about being a stand-up comic at your age is standing up. I know you're old—a fortune-teller I know offered to read your face."

MICKEY ROONEY: "I knew you were getting older when you played the slot machine and it came out three prunes."

PHYLLIS DILLER: "I've had a crush on George for years. He's my kind of guy—he's handsome, he's successful—and he's breathing."

HOWARD COSELL: "Of course George is against sin—he's against anything he's too old to enjoy."

HENNY YOUNGMAN: "He's at the age where his back goes out more than he does."

WARREN BEATTY asked me what he could talk about. I said, "You could talk about five mintes—could you talk about his sex life?" He said, "Sure, but what will I talk about the other four minutes?"

I love George Burns. He's part of the history of this country and the world—but it's not true he was a waiter at the Last Supper.

Hail from the Chief, RONALD REAGAN: "I just couldn't turn down the opportunity to say a few words about George Burns, this bionic geriatric, this Sun City Fonzie. George Burns . . . the only man who does fool Mother Nature. George, Nancy wanted me to tell you that you're her favorite singer. But then, Harry Truman was her favorite piano player. Just the other night, I thought she had one of your records on. It turned out to be a spoon caught in the garbage disposal. But seriously, George, who else do you know who was an actual eyewitness to most of the history of our country? It was George Burns who told Betsy Ross, 'Personally, I feel the pattern's a little busy—but let's run it up the flagpole and see if anybody salutes.' "

We all love him. CAROL CHANNING says, "He knew the Statue of Liberty when she was a little girl." Listen, he MC'd Peter Minuet's bar mitzvah. When the pilgrims landed on Plymouth Rock, it was toastmaster Burns who said, "A funny thing happened on the way to the *Mayflower*."

All his pals were there to salute him on his birthday. FRANK SINATRA toasted, "Old? When he was growing up people used to refer to the flag as Young Glory." RED BUTTONS noted, "When he was a young man, cigarette packages carried a warning from the surgeon corporal." FREDDIE ROMAN said, "He's getting a little too old for break dancing—his idea of sex is to cuddle with a hot water bottle." SAMMY DAVIS, JR.: "Even as a kid George had charisma—then he started dating girls and his charisma cleared up."

DANNY THOMAS pleaded with George: "I wish you would slow down—so we could all keep up with you." "I can't slow down," George explained. "I'm booked through 1995."

George explained, "It's great to get old—especially in the winter. Everybody comes to your birthday party and they stand around the cake just to get warm."

Frank Sinatra

MILTON BERLE said to Sinatra: "If your zipper could only talk."

DON RICKLES remarked: "Don't just sit there, Frank, enjoy yourself—hit somebody."

HOWARD COSELL purred: "Sinatra is an antique relic of yesteryear—he is the Paul Anka of the menopause set."

That's the way it is with the world-famous theatrical club, the Friars—they do you in to do you proud. They came from all over the world, not to praise the emperor, but to bury him.

So Sinatra is a little temperamental—so he declared war on New Jersey, so he flattened a few critics . . .

BERLE hollered, "I'll tell you one thing about Sinatra. No one has ever been turned away from his door—if you're over twenty-one and have big knockers."

DON RICKLES: "Everything Sinatra touches turns to gold. I'm afraid to go to the toilet with him."

Sinatra dredged out CARY GRANT, MILTON BERLE, ROBERT MERRILL, JAN MURRAY, DON RICKLES, Mayor ABE BEAME, Governor HUGH CAREY, SARAH VAUGHAN, ED McMAHON, JOHN DENVER, FRANK SINATRA, JR., and a ton and a half of other celebrities stamped U.S. Prime. MILTON BERLE summed it up: "We are all here for one reason and one reason only. You can sum it up in one word: *fear.*"

JAN MURRAY said: "Invitations were extended to this dinner for Frank in an unusual fashion. A guy drove up in a cement truck and asked me for my shoe size."

BERLE noted: "What a crowd! I would say mob—but you know how sensitive Frank is. This aging JERRY VALE is very charitable. He built the Eisenhower Hospital in Palm Springs—and put all his friends in it."

CARY GRANT said: "On my feet I cease to function. To tell the truth, I can't function when I'm lying down either—that's why I love your style, Frank."

"What's all the fuss about this elderly BOBBY VINTON?" HOWARD COSELL wanted to know. "He's a grandfather. And the kid is just like him. The first photo made of the new grandchild, the kid slugged the photographer."

Milton added that Frank made it the hard way: "He came from a little town. The town was so small the local hooker was a virgin."

"Frank has never let anything put him down. Once he went to visit a little old man in a hospital in Hoboken and he sang to the poor soul for an hour. When he was finished he said to him: 'I hope you get better.' And the little old man said, 'You too!' "

"I'll tell you how big Sinatra is," DON RICKLES said, "he

wears a cross in nobody's honor." Don said: "When you enter the room you have to kiss his ring. I don't mind—but he has it in his back pocket."

DEAN MARTIN: "Frank lent money to New York. When they didn't repay, he broke the Statue of Liberty's arms."

Dean noted: "Frank's best friend couldn't be here—he's on a hook in New Jersey."

"Half of Frank's pals couldn't be here. Half couldn't find the time and the other half are doing time. But Frank's the king. He speaks to God on a one-to-one basis.

"Frank calls Dial-a-Prayer to see if he has any messages."

RED BUTTONS: "Frank was born in a tough neighborhood in Hoboken. You could walk ten miles and never leave the scene of the crime."

LUCILLE BALL: "Frank Sinatra leads a full, exciting life . . . never a dull moment. Even when he went to church, four or five priests would crowd into the confessional booth. It isn't often that a confession gets applause."

GEORGE BURNS: "When Sinatra plays Las Vegas all the beautiful women in the audience throw their hotel keys up on the stage. When I play there women throw their room keys at me, too—but after they check out."

Comedian PAT HENRY took note of the $500-a-plate charge and said he'd ask for a doggy bag to take home leftovers. "But I'm not walking through my neighborhood with $400 worth of meat."

Pat praised his idol as a family man: "And he thinks of

the press as family. How often I have heard Sinatra say to JILLY RIZZO, 'Get rid of these mothers.' "

"I'm sorry BOB HOPE couldn't be here," BERLE told us, "but something came up and he was very proud."

DON RICKLES was sentimental: "We have an understanding that if there's gunshots, I stand still while he ducks."

"Sinatra is a perfectionist," I told them. "Sure, I know a lot of people who sing in a shower—but when Frank showers, he takes a backup band in there with him."

Of course, it was the biggest turnout of all time—and the Friars have been roasting the biggest names at these dinners since the Last Supper. JEAN-PIERRE TREBOT, the executive director of the Friars, told me even Judas didn't sell as many tickets as our Frank.

As I said proudly, "Frank is more than a friend to me—he's a total stranger."

RED BUTTONS spoke up: "As Frank said to MARGARET THATCHER, 'Your fly is open.' "

ALAN KING said, "Sinatra is the only American who is in *Who's Who* and the *Kinsey Report* at the same time."

Sinatra's generosity was emphasized. How he gives away a fortune. Once in Las Vegas Frank saw a bent-over old man emptying ashtrays in the casino and he threw him four $100 bills. The little old man said, "Keep your money, schmuck. I'm trying to clean up my hotel—I'm HOWARD HUGHES."

JAN MURRAY: "Frank invited me to live here at the Waldorf

with him. 'Live my life,' he said. My heart said yes but my prostate said no.''

ED McMAHON said, ''Frank speaks to God, not in prayer but as a consultant. Sinatra almost didn't make it here tonight— he was taking a walk and was hit by a motorboat.''

''McMAHON has a lot of talent,'' Milton said, ''But it's in JOHNNY CARSON's name.''

CARSON said, ''I don't know if you heard about it, but Ed likes to take a drink once in a while. In fact, I didn't know he was a drinker until he came to work sober one night.'' Johnny said, ''Sinatra had a great television show. It was canceled—the critics thought it was good, but word of mouth killed it.''

RICKLES closed it well: ''You got a great voice, Frank—too bad it hasn't reached your throat.''

RONALD REAGAN called to say, ''Frank, you're my favorite star—next to Bonzo.''

Sinatra said it all: ''I thank you all. You know, my father wasn't born in this country, but I thank him for making sure that I was born in this blessed America. My fellow Friars and friends—put me down for a favor. I owe each and every one of you. I give you my marker.''

Pearl Bailey

It's not easy to roast a gal—I told that to Pearl Bailey when I was asked to be her hangman when the March of Dimes put her up for slaughter. "If you spare the rod," she cracked, "I'll never forgive you. If I can dish it out, I can take it." It was tough, but how can you refuse such an invitation,

"We are honoring Pearl Bailey," I started, "because she's a great star—the First Lady of Broadway—and the NAACP insisted.

"She was always a regular at the White House. When Lady Bird left, Pearl told her not to worry—she could always come in and work for her Tuesdays and Thursdays.

"If she becomes Jewish, I'll make her a star—then she and SAMMY DAVIS can open their own synagogue.

"She had it tough in the old days, when she was a little girl in Shanghai—Shanghai? Pardon me—that's a line left over from an old Pearl *Buck* dinner."

"This is a classy girl, this Pearl Bailey. When she didn't get the picture for *Hello, Dolly!* she made no fuss. GINGER

ROGERS whimpered, CAROL CHANNING cried, but not a word from Pearl. She did have the boys from the NAACP do a little picketing."

Milton Berle

Milton, who billed himself as "The Thief of Bad Gags," laughed himself well when I brought his own stolen gems back to him at the hospital:

When women go wrong, men go right after them.

He told her he wanted some old-fashioned loving, so she introduced him to her grandmother.

You've reached middle age when you know your way around but you'd rather not go.

With the peek-a-boo dresses, the see-through blouses, and the mini-skirts, there is no longer any such thing as a blind date.

Honesty is the best policy—but not the best politics.

Just think of all the men in this country who dream of marrying one of the GABORS—and do.

Some of the quiz shows and game shows on TV are getting

ridiculous. I know a nine-year-old kid who had to get married because he won a honeymoon vacation for two in Hawaii.

Milton said to BOB HOPE: "Here's a joke that will crack you up." Hope said, "I heard it." Berle said, "How do you know, I haven't told it yet." Hope said, "If you're telling it, I heard it."

HENNY YOUNGMAN said to a nine-year-old, "You should take violin lessons and someday you'll play like I do." Milton interrupted. "You mean you had to take lessons to play like you do?"

Milton told me, "I tried to use my Mastercharge in a health food store and the clerk told me they only accept natural cash." Berle's comment on DOLLY PARTON: "She was in a national magazine and they couldn't close the magazine over the centerfold."

Berle swears this "lady" approached him on Broadway and said, "Mister, can you lend me $50 till I get back on my back."

Milton says: "One thing, I have great respect for girls. Only last week in New York, I saved a girl from being attacked—I controlled myself." "I think I'm getting a little old now: I just asked the Good Humor man for a prune Popsicle."

DICK SHAWN raved about Milton: "I saw your television show last night and you were never funnier—and it's a shame."

DICK CAVETT challenged Milton to a battle of wits. Berle said, "I'll check my brains and we'll start even." Dick answered, "Where will you be able to get such a small size checkroom?" Dick said, "If REAGAN can go to Germany, I hear Berle will go to England and put a wreath on the grave of Jack the Ripper."

SAMMY DAVIS, JR., sang out: "I love him. I don't want to say he's getting old, but the other day he went to a porno movie and fell asleep."

BARBARA WALTERS declared, "I've admired Milton for years—none of them recently."

Milton reminded me that Barbara was writing a documentary: *Poland—Gateway to the Orient.*

It was HAL KANTER who summed it all up: "Milton Berle has given us more laughs than MARIA OUSPENSKAYA, RICHARD NIXON, and Attila the Hun combined."

I told Berle at the finish: "Remember, Milton, this is all done in the name of friendship. We always roast the ones we love—and if you believe that, I have a condominium in Lebanon I'd like to unload on you."

Burt Reynolds

JOHNNY CARSON was the roastmaster, "Ladies and gentlemen, we are here tonight for one common purpose, to watch Burt Reynolds give the finest acting performance of the year—when he fakes being humble."

MICKEY ROONEY was loving: "Burt Reynolds is giving up his career to become an actor."

Burt has always said, "I prefer a girl who's sexy, not brainy—when I feel intellectual I can always go to the public library."

DON RICKLES said: "Burt, in my book you have the sexual attractiveness of a dentist's drill."

DINAH SHORE was a little more understanding. "When the history of this particular age is recorded it will be in the books that Burt Reynolds has done more for little old ladies in tennis shoes than anyone else in this world."

"Burt told me: 'The eyes are the first to go. In my case the second. My hair went first. It's not all gone. Some of it is in a drawer up in the room.'

I said: "Burt doesn't give a second thought to women—his first thought covers everything.

"Burt Reynolds is a big star. I know, because before the dinner he came up to me and told me, 'I'm a big star.'

"He's always had a great way with the ladies. It's expensive, but it's a way.

"I hear Burt has finally found true romance—he's in love with himself again. His new book is selling for $10.95—autographed, $3.75.

"I hear the President is going to name him to a cabinet post: Secretary of the Inferior.

"His version of the Golden Rule is simple: 'Do unto others.' "

"Of course," CARSON confided, "even he will tell you he's not the same sexpert he was when he posed for the centerfold in the nude, with the largest hand in show business. Don't misunderstand—they still want him for the centerfold of a magazine—*Popular Mechanics*. They tell me that in a forthcoming issue of *Cosmopolitan* HOWARD COSELL will be the centerfold, with his vital organ covered—his mouth."

HOWARD COSELL cried: "Burt is always amazed at his sexy reputation. If he did a quarter of the things he's accused of or credited with, he'd be in a jar at Harvard."

At the dinner they were discussing Burt's love life. "Poor guy," said ALAN KING, "one year he's making love to a JULIE ANDREWS, a LONI ANDERSON, a DOLLY PARTON—next year he's a has-been." GEORGE BURNS said, "Yeah, but look where he has been."

DAVID STEINBERG: "People wonder what Burt Reynolds and I have in common. There is so much. Burt's father is a sheriff. My father is a rabbi. We often discussed what our fathers told us. My father taught me that Gentiles, though intelligent, sell their children for whiskey.

"Burt would make a great Jew. He's warm and sensitive and he's completely guilt-ridden. Of course, if he was a Jew he never would have become a stunt man. Because 'stunt man' in Yiddish is *schumuck*."

Steinberg introduced CHARLES NELSON REILLY: "The only man I know who can make a Valium nervous. ROBERT YOUNG goes to his house to rehearse his Sanka commercial."

Charles said, "Burt Reynolds can look at a girl's future and tell what kind of past she's going to have. Burt is a great help to all causes—he responds to most appeals—but his favorite charity is still the sex drive."

When he sat down, Johnny said, "Thank you, Charles, for getting things off to a flying stop."

Johnny said, "Burt has often been compared to CLARK GABLE—A Clark Gable he's not."

I added, "Yeah? Well, I heard that Mr. Reynolds is now testing for the old Clark Gable parts. The only trouble is, his old parts don't work as well as Gable's did."

To quote Burt Reynolds: "Marriage is about the most expensive way for the average man to get his laundry done."

Johnny explained: "Burt Reynolds insists his new movie, *The Man Who Loved Women*, is not autobiographical, but he admits he did help with research on the script."

The Man Who Loved Women was produced and directed by BLAKE EDWARDS and co-starred Mrs. Edwards, JULIE AN-DREWS. Burt loved making it. He said, "In what other business would a guy pay you to make love to his wife, show you how to do it, and make you do it over again and again until you get it right."

Burt's thank you speech was about his favorite subject. "I didn't invent sex. Show me a man who says 'I love you' to his lady in the morning—and I'll show you a man getting dressed to go home. When a woman tells you she doesn't mess around with a married man, she means her husband."

JOHNNY CARSON closed with one bit of advice to Burt and all his swinger fans: "While waiting for the right partner to come along, have a ball with the wrong ones."

Dean Martin

Roastmaster **FRANK SINATRA**: "We are paying tribute to a man who does not even know he's here—singer, actor, comedian, raconteur, drunk. I asked him once, 'Why don't we go down to Disneyland? We haven't been there in twenty years.' He looked at me: 'With my hallucinations, I *am* Disneyland.' " Dean said, "I am suffering from my first hangover." Sinatra asked, "How long have you had it?" Dean said, "Since 1927."

SHIRLEY MACLAINE: "I've known Dean Martin for thirty years. He's been friend, confidant, and someone I could call at any hour of the night—pour out my heart to him and know with real certainty that he would not remember a thing in the morning."

MILTON BERLE: "**HENNY YOUNGMAN**, wherever you're sitting, if there's a fire in this place tonight, we leave the room alphabetically. I'm not going to stay on too long—and if you believe that, you'll also believe there's also a Liberace Junior."

"I've become an author and written four of the shortest books in the world: *Famous Jewish Astronauts, 10,000 Years of German Humor, Irish Gourmet Cooking,* and *Blacks I Have Met While Yachting.*

"SINATRA works with kings and plays with queens, as long as they're dealt by hand.

"Sinatra—a man so powerful that his birthplace is now listed as Hoboken, Connecticut.

"Sinatra was so nervous that to pacify him I gave him my favorite Jewish good luck charm—a rabbi's foot.

"Waiting for Dean Martin to stop drinking is like leaving the porch light on for JIMMY HOFFA.

"I don't like to talk about age. I just want to live long enough to see who winds up with BROOKE SHIELDS.

"Dino has done a lot for the Jews, just by not being one.

"The Italians and the Jews have a lot in common. It was an Italian who invented the toilet seat—but it was a Jew who had brains enough to put a hole in it.

"L'chaim—I'd like to make a toast for the Friars' eightieth birthday. For the very few who don't know what *l'chaim* means, it means life—in fact, Dino has a cousin who is doing *l'chaim* in San Quentin."

LUCILLE BALL: "The Friars bestowed an honor on me many years ago as the first lady to be honored. JOHNNY CARSON was the master of ceremonies. The committee told him that ladies as well as gentlemen would be in the audience and please do not be off-color. Johnny Carson gets up to the microphone and says: 'What a thrill it is to present Miss Lucille Testicle.'

"Dean gave up six nights of his valuable time to personally tutor GEORGE BURNS in a refresher course on sex.

"Dean is founder of the antiabstinence league and has adopted his own slogan, "Good health is bad for you.""

"He made a grant to Johns Hopkins University for a Teflon liver.

"On the Bowery every New Year's Eve, Dean quietly places a wreath on the tomb of the unknown drunk."

DICK SHAWN: "Think of Frank, Sammy, and Dean together. There isn't one man that at one time hasn't said; I wish I had what these three guys have—except for their livers. Three of the worst livers in show biz.

"Jews cannot sing. TONY MARTIN when his name was Al Morris could not sing. He changed his name, sang "The Cohens, The Kellys," and became a singer. SAMMY DAVIS, JR., had eighty gold records until he became Jewish, hasn't had a record since.

"One good thing about a tribute and not a roast, where you attack, is that everything you say can be said again—at his funeral."

Tribute to SAMMY DAVIS: "For Sammy's fiftieth anniversary in show biz, fifty was his lucky number—fifty members on the dais—$50,000 a night—but he is only fifty inches tall.

"GEORGE BURNS—in show biz for seventy years. Think of that. Incredible when you consider that Yugoslavia is only forty-eight years old. He's older than Yugoslavia.

"All comics have a problem these days. You have to work dirty. New play won a Pulitzer Prize—mention a dirty word 240 times, it becomes literature. You have to talk to young people with the language of today. RICHARD PRYOR, GEORGE CARLIN. If that's what they want to hear—fuck 'em."

RED BUTTONS: "We're giving Dean Martin a dinner—seems a little silly: GUCCI—who said, 'He who steals my purse should buy a pair of shoes to match'—never got a dinner. RICHARD PRYOR—who said to the Olympic committee, 'Ain't no way this mother's gonna carry that torch'—never got a dinner. Moses—who said when he came down from Mount Sinai, 'The food in that hospital is terrible'—never got a dinner. John Wilkes Booth—who said, 'I'm sorry. I thought he was a critic'—never got a dinner. Cain—whose wife divorced him—'cause he wasn't able—never got a dinner. Saint Francis—whose own father called him a sissy—never got a dinner. GERALDINE FERRARO—who said, 'This is the last time I go to H. & R. Block'—never got a dinner. DR. SPOCK—who said, 'Never raise your hands to your kids—it leaves your groin unprotected'—never got a dinner."

Red was now screaming: "MARTIN VAN BUREN, in order not to come late to his inauguration, slept with a rooster. MILTON BERLE: Wonderful man—a man who went to the funeral and stole the eulogy."

Red hollered, "Dean is everywhere. In Harlem at a rally of Black Hockey Players for Reagan—he was there. In Tehran at an Iranian massage parlor during happy hour, where deep-breathing ayatollahs blow-dry each other's beards—he was there. In Biloxi, Mississippi, at a Rinso White Ku Klux Klan rally—he was there. In Tokyo at a reunion of Japanese Kamikaze pilots—their motto is 'We may be yellow, but we're not shmucks'—the man was there. In Nigeria at an exhibition of Hasidic male strippers who love to undress and show their tsitsis—the man was there. In Nantucket at a culmination of seafaring rabbis who believed that Captain Ahab only wanted to circumcise Moby Dick—the man was there."

GREG GARISON: "If Dean stopped working today, he would be financially set for the rest of his life. His investment's being handled by GERALDINE FERRARO's husband.

"**JOHNNY CARSON'S** first wife was Joan, second wife was Joanne, third wife was Joanna. I don't want to say he's cheap, but the man will do anything not to buy new towels.

"Dean Martin suggested a great recipe for a Christmas turkey: 'Take a fifteen-pound turkey, pour on one quart of Scotch, heat it, then pour a quart of gin over it, then a quart of Burgundy, then put it back in the oven for one hour. Then you take the turkey out of the oven and throw it out the window—but oh, what a gravy.' "

BOB HOPE revealed: "Dean Martin told me he's considering filling his swimming pool with martinis. He claims that'll make it impossible to drown, since the deeper you sink, the higher you'll get."

Dean tells me the staff of the Golden Nugget in Las Vegas are very considerate: "The morning after they always serve my breakfast on the floor."

I said, "I love Dean Martin—I wish he were alive to enjoy this tribute.

"He's so literate—he established a fellowship in the name of **PIA ZADORA**.

"The astronaut is the second highest man has been—Dean Martin still holds the record.

"You know, that's a big lie about how much Dean drinks. I know him a long time and I never saw him take a drink until dinnertime. In fact, last week I had dinner at his house and you never saw such a banquet—but who can eat that much at eight o'clock in the morning?"

Dean said to me: "Joey, I like you—when I'm drinking I like anybody."

Frank told us: "Dean ordered a martini from the waiter, 'extra rare.' The waiter corrected, 'You mean extra dry.' Dean said, 'No extra rare—I'm having it for dinner."

HENNY YOUNGMAN was screaming, "Dean, if you had your life to live over again—do it overseas.

"Dean told me, 'If it weren't for pretzels and peanuts, I'd be on a liquid diet.'

JOHNNY CARSON: "Dean is the most relaxed performer on television—he never spills a word. Dean is never as drunk as he appears—he's drunker."

Before the dinner I asked Dean, "What kind of person are you?" He answered, "I really don't know—because nobody's told me."

BROOKE SHIELDS said, "What can you say about Dean Martin that hasn't been said about Old Grandad?"

SAMMY DAVIS, JR.: "Dean isn't drinking anymore. He isn't drinking any less, either."

ANGIE DICKINSON: "Sex makes the world go round. Dean feels whiskey will do the same thing much cheaper."

President REAGAN sent a wire: "You're an inspiration to all singers. They figure if *you* can make it, anybody can."

Dean answered everybody lovingly: "I'll give you some wonderful tips on drinking—because you have been so nice to me. Most drinkers don't think it's a sin—they're proud of it. Sinatra tells me he likes his booze on the rocks—I like mine on land, sea, or on a plane. One way to cut down on drunk driving would be for the saloons to offer free home delivery. To avoid a hangover, keep drinking. Everybody, have a drink on me. I'm drunk—do I know what I'm saying?"

ROAST
of the
TOWN

Elizabeth Taylor
Hilton Wilding
Todd Fisher
Burton Burton
Warner . . .

Roastmaster DINAH SHORE took the first shot: "It may not be apparent to the naked eye, but Elizabeth Taylor and I have a lot in common—We both like jewelry. It's just a question of size. We both have a thing about actors, and again it's just a question of size.

"As Maggie in *Cat on a Hot Tin Roof* she did for a slip what Tom Selleck is now doing for the T-shirt.

"For her brilliant performance in *Who's Afraid of Virginia Woolf* she not only went to the play, studied the script, and studied the manuscript, she spent hours watching SHELLEY WINTERS talking to her agent."

The real target of the evening was JOAN RIVERS. Dinah

noted: "JEAN-PIERRE TREBOT, the director of the Friars, told me that the gold tables here tonight go for $10,000, the platinum tables go for $7,500, and the silver tables go for $5,000. Now if there are any of you here tonight who would like to see Joan Rivers and her husband, you can go over to Lexington Avenue for the Formica table."

All Joan said was, "Liz is so fat—her favorite food is seconds; she goes through a revolving door in two trips."

Liz said: "Talk about big mouth—when Joan yawns, her entire face disappears."

BUDDY HACKETT: "You might be interested in hearing about what happened to Joan Rivers last night—a peeping Tom threw up on her window."

On Elizabeth Taylor: "Any man within the sound of my voice or in this entire universe who has never fantasized about Elizabeth Taylor is either gay or an agent."

"I have tried to pattern my career after her. You'll notice I have never had George Hamilton as a leading man."

ROD McKUEN: "Last year Joan Rivers was gang-banged by all the New York critics and nobody wants the pick of the litter."

ROGER MOORE: "Joan Rivers is the depressed area's DON RICKLES . . . only not quite as pretty. The largest thing in America today is Joan River's tongue."

ROBERT KLEIN on Elizabeth Taylor: "I feel my accomplishments pale before our honoree. I was on *What's My Line* near the end of its tenure and it was so pathetic. I was the mystery guest and they didn't get me. Then they took off their blindfolds and they still didn't get me.

"My wife is an opera singer and starting to make a living at it. It's a switch after all those years of money for lessons and all. Now she makes money at it. Europe, Paris, Amsterdam, Covent Garden. And she brings me the checks. And it makes me feel good. Like an opera pimp . . . 'Where's that money from that *Rigoletto*?' "

I introduced HENRY KISSINGER: "He can always be depended on to accept a speaking invitation—he's accepted more proposals than Elizabeth Taylor."

CARY GRANT: "Elizabeth is writing a book about her boyfriends—she's now up to chapter forty-six."

DENNIS STEIN said: "They say the human body is ninety-two percent water. I don't ask for much—all I want is Elizabeth Taylor and a straw."

FRANK SINATRA: "Tonight we talk about the lives and loves of Elizabeth Taylor. Relax, folks we're going to be here a long time!"

I said, "Baseball is our national pastime—now go convince Elizabeth Taylor. Liz is more to be petted than censored—we should pray for her." One guy yelled out, "I've been praying for her for years, but I never got her."

"She no longer gets a marriage license—she just pencils in the name of her latest husband on a slate. She could save a lot of time if she'd just keep the bouquet and throw the groom away.

"I think Liz has made a real success of marriage—she's the first to do it as a series. Liz got married seven times and got richer by decrees. She feels a woman should get married for love, and she should keep on getting married until she finds it.

"Liz's big disappointment was that she didn't get a Tony award on Broadway—because she never had a Tony. She had a Nicky, a Michael, a Mike, and an Eddie, a couple of Richards, and a John—but never a Tony."

RED BUTTONS hollered, "A dinner for Elizabeth Taylor? Some of the biggest people in the world never got a dinner. MAHATMA GHANDI's mother—who said, 'Eat a cookie, who's gonna know?'—never got a dinner. STEVEN SPIELBERG's mother—who said to ET, 'I don't care where you're from, you're going to get bar mitzvahed'—never got a dinner.

"JOHN DELOREAN—who has a real nose for business—never got a dinner. King Henry VIII—who said to his lawyer, 'Forget the alimony, I got a better idea'—never got a dinner. Abraham Lincoln—who said a house divided is a condominium—never ... Moses—who said to the children of Israel 'Stop calling me Charlton,'—he never got a dinner. Jesus—who never got a dinner so they gave Him a supper—never ... Queen Elizabeth—who almost had a heart attack when she thought it was Phillip who was sitting on the bed ... Santa Claus's mother—who said, 'Since he got into the toy business he's never home for Chankuh'—never got a dinner."

Elizabeth Taylor—who is right now building a halfway house for girls who don't want to go all the way ...

Liz said it all: "Show me a man who doesn't put a price on love—and I'll show you a man who hasn't paid alimony.

"It is impossible for a woman to be married to the same man for any long period of time. In just a short time, he's not the same man."

Well, as Elizabeth said when she called up her bridesmaids, "It's time to get back to work."

ZSA ZSA added: "A woman should get married for love, and she should keep on getting married till she finds it."

So I said, "Elizabeth Taylor is getting married again. Everyone has a hobby—some people collect stamps.

"With all the famous people at her doorstep, Elizabeth Taylor asked *me* out. I was in her apartment at the time."

JACK PAAR said it: "Elizabeth Taylor should get a divorce and settle down."

JOAN RIVERS about Elizabeth Taylor: "I won't say she's fat, but she had a face lift and there was enough skin left over to make another person."

Liz about Joan: "She says she's touching fifty. Touching it? She's beating the hell out of it."

Joan about Liz: "You know you're getting old and fat when your age and waistline are the same number.

"Liz fat? During her vacation in Florida she was ejected from a local beach for creating too much shade.

"Fat? She wore a gray dress and an admiral tried to board her.

"Fat? She has to wear two girdles—an upper and a lower.

"Fat? She qualifies for group insurance.

"Fat? What a body—I think she models for beer kegs.

"The only exercise she does is eating.

"It was so embarrassing—I took her to Sea World. Shamu the Whale jumped up out of the water, and Liz asked if it came with vegetables."

John Lindsay

When Lindsay was Mayor of New York City he called me every other day for jokes for his appearances. I was toastmaster at one dinner for him, and again he called for the necessary lines to make him witty again. I gave him eight great jokes. I also rehearsed him in his lines and delivery. Right before I introduced him I did all the eight jokes.

I hate to admit it, but John topped me. He said, "I met Joey Adams in the men's room right before the dinner and he was nervous as hell. He said this was a show-business dinner and he wasn't prepared with any material. He was actually crying. I felt sorry for him, so I gave him all my jokes. You just heard them—so good night and thank you!"

Comedy, in order to be effective, must be devastating—you must deliver the lines as though you mean it. When you insert the scalpel, you can't dull the edge by saying "I'm only joking"; you've got to stick with your incisions.

At a dinner for Cardinal O'Connor, I said, "Talking about the Pill, your Eminence—if you don't play the game, don't make the rules" and I said it as though I meant it.

Of course, we play it strictly for laughs. We don't want to leave any scars. DON RICKLES claims only one person ever objected to his needling: "I made fun of a ringsider's beard and almost got belted—that broad had no sense of humor."

Howard Cosell

"Howard Cosell must be slipping—in his book he forgot to attack Saint Francis and Mother Theresa.

"He's got a $20 bill and a shirt and he never changes either.

"You know, if he ever lost face, it would be an improvement.

"With the cost of living so high, why does he bother?

"I always said he would make it—and I still say he's going to make it."

Rodney Dangerfield

"As a kid his folks didn't exactly love him—they gave him his allowance in traveler's checks.

"May his sex life be as good as his credit.

"He's into acupuncture—in bars he's always sticking people for drinks.

"EDDIE FISHER was once married to ELIZABETH TAYLOR. That's like trying to wash down the Empire State Building with one bar of soap.

"Rodney's going to live to be an unknown.

"His wife practices the rhythm method—that means she won't make love unless there's a drummer in the room.

"He was an ugly kid. Every time his father wanted sex, his mother showed him Rodney's picture.

"We have two disappointments tonight: BOB HOPE couldn't make it, and JOHNNY CARSON could.

"He asked his wife, 'What can I do to get you more interested in sex?' She said, 'Leave town!'

"He's trying to find himself—and when he does, he's a cinch to be disappointed. Mean? He's the inventor of the exact-change ambulance. Cheap? Who else do you know goes to a massage parlor on standby?"

Don Rickles

"You're a nice-looking guy, Don. Of course, if I had a head like that, I'd have it circumcised.

"I overheard Don in a conversation between him and another guy in the john, and apparently there was no paper. So Don was banging on the door next to him, saying, 'Hey, buddy, you got any paper over there?' The guy said, 'No, I haven't got any.' So Don says, 'Well, have you got change for a ten?'

"Don has a rather bad kidney problem. You can tell by his rusty zipper and his yellow tennis shoes.

"Don is the living proof of the desirability of constant use of contraceptives."

Jack Klugman

TONY RANDALL: "I admit that Jack is less than perfect. But let me tell you something. There is a justification for everything he does. Sure, he goes around with his shirttails hanging out in front . . . but there's a reason for it. His fly is usually open."

MILTON BERLE: "Let me tell you what kind of guy Jack Klugman is. When he goes to a party, nobody says hello. But when he leaves, everybody says good-bye."

DEAN MARTIN: Though Jack Klugman has appeared on Broadway, television, and motion pictures, he is the most underrated talent in show business . . . and deservedly so."

KAY MEDFORD: "On *Quincy*, Jack plays a coroner at the morgue, and he's always poking his head under a sheet. Jack, you look like the manager of a motel telling a couple that their hour is up."

Henny
Youngman

The Friars roast for HENNY YOUNGMAN was historical if not hysterical. "Youngman," said Berle, "was born in London, of poor but stupid parents."

I said, "Youngman, who was so popular years ago, is able to tell twenty-three jokes in as many seconds—mainly because he is never interrupted by laughs."

FREDDIE ROMAN spoke of Henny's musical talents: "When he opened his violin case, many hoped a machine gun would be in there.

PHIL SILVERS said,"Henny had about as much chance of getting his own TV show as BOY GEORGE has of becoming father of the year."

GENE BAYLOS: "I wish he were as well known as his jokes."

JACKIE VERNON: "He's not too smart—the only book he ever finished was a book of matches."

MOREY AMSTERDAM: "He's so well known, he's been getting a lot of TV work—all his friends bring him their TV sets to fix."

Henny was very gracious: "I'm giving a dinner party next week for all my friends." BERLE hollered out, "Dining alone, eh?"

Henny said, "I'm at the age now where I need friends. If it weren't for pickpockets, I would have no sex life at all."

I introduced Milton Berle to present his protégé and pal Henny Youngman. "Henny," said Miltie, "is one of the great comedians of our generation. This is not only my opinion—it's Henny's.

"I've known Henny Youngman, man and joke file, for over forty years. Unlike myself, Henny did not steal jokes from the top comedians of that era. Henny stole from the unknowns—a word which later became synonymous with his career.

"The greatest form of flattery is imitation—and one of Henny's unusual traits is that he is flattered by the fact that for many years he has been an imitation of a comedian.

"Actually, I kid a lot about Henny—but the truth is he is the fastest comedian around. He has to be with his act.

"Ladies and gentlemen, I give you Henny Youngman—and you can have him."

HENNY YOUNGMAN: "I just finished filling out my income tax form. Who said you can't get wounded by a blank? Which reminds me—a drunk walked up to a parking meter and put in a dime. The dial went to 60. He said, 'How about that—I lost 100 pounds.' "

Earl Wilson

Earl Wilson was roasted by the Friars as the Bust Columnist in town.

As Earl said about his friend **DOLLY PARTON**: "The bigger they are, the nicer they are."

Since he's my best friend, I started it: "He once drove a cab—he must have, he's a hack writer." I was proud to tell him, "I think you're the second greatest writer—second only to the guy who writes on bathroom walls with a spray can."

GEORGIE JESSEL lauded Earl: "His scoops are numerous. He was first with the news that Lynda Bird Johnson was marrying George Hamilton. Last year somebody told him about World War II and he printed it as a rumor. He is a familiar figure at all nightclub openings, sleeping soundly at a ringside table. He is a great audience for comedians because, compared to him, Ed Sullivan is a laughing hyena. He discovered many busty starlets and made unknowns out of them."

Ed Sullivan

As roastmaster at the March of Dimes roast of Ed Sullivan, I took the first slice: "When it was announced that this was a dinner for the great columnist and TV host Ed Sullivan, everybody hollered at once—*why?*' "

ED SULLIVAN was a small-town boy from Portchester, New York, who was a sportswriter and columnist for the *Evening Mail*, the *Graphic*, and finally the *Daily News* before he went on TV to become the number one host of all the networks. He wasn't a comedian or wit—or even a good master of ceremonies. He was a good *pointer*—but he pointed to the biggest stars and greatest comics. He found most of them at the Friars and Lambs Club Round Tables—and from among the comics who submitted their best jokes for his column.

GEORGIE JESSEL: "I wouldn't say Ed has no personality—but his TV show is in color and he comes out in black-and-white.

"I have never known anyone who was the recipient of a dinner who didn't have something that was pretty good. No one ever gave a dinner to Hitler, Al Capone, or Sitting Bull.

"One thing you can be sure—there's never a dull moment when Ed is on the air. It lasts the entire show.

"The secret of his success—still is."

JOAN RIVERS: "I was on the Ed Sullivan show and had to follow an elephant—and had to share a dressing room with the elephant. Ed came to the dressing room and apologized for putting us together. 'Oh, that's all right,' I said humbly. 'I wasn't talking to you,' Ed snapped."

PETER LIND HAYES: "He's the only golfer who falls asleep in his own backswing."

JAN MURRAY: "Ed knows what the public likes—and one of these days he's going to give it to them."

PAUL FORD: "I first met Ed Sullivan at the Actors Studio. He was their first dropout. Later on he learned how to mumble by himself."

BOB HOPE: "The truth is Ed cares about giving new people a chance on his television show. It was Ed who first started the one and only Bella Magdowitz. It was Ed and Ed alone who gave the first opportunity to Sylvia Cocktepple—and the Fiji Island Drum and Fife Corps.
"Ed has taken some of the biggest stars and made unknowns of them.
"It was Vincent Lopez who first predicted Ed would be our biggest TV personality in the twentieth century—but he also predicted ZSA ZSA GABOR would become a nun.

"This man has been on the same network—CBS—for over twenty years. You know why? No other network wanted him.

"A lot of people say he has a lousy personality. That's not

ROAST
of the
TOWN

121

true—he has no personality at all. He has that unusual some-thing that brightens a room when he leaves it.

"Where else could Ed go from here? He's been a sports-writer, columnist, TV star, movie actor. Some people say he should do what GEORGE MURPHY and RONALD REGAN did—get the hell out of show business."

Jack Benny

At one party for Jack Benny, the dais was loaded with stars waiting to explode. I started the fireworks: "Any man who needs so many character witnesses shouldn't be a guest of honor.

"We wanted to make this a great party for Jack. We thought about digging up some of his old friends—and we'd have to—like Aaron Burr, Attila the Hun, DOUGLAS FAIRBANKS SENIOR's father, and the ever popular MAE BUSCH.

"He brought his violin with him tonight—and he may play for us—but I'm sorry his original piano player couldn't be with us—Ludwig van Beethoven—or his old brother Isaiah.

"I think Jack is one of the funniest violin players in the world—he has the only Stradivarius made in Japan.

"All I can tell you is HENNY YOUNGMAN ain't got to worry. In fact, Venus de Milo could play better."

GEORGE BURNS: "It's appropriate that we give Jack Benny a dinner—everybody does. He hasn't picked up a check in thirty years.

"You can always recognize Jack—sitting with his back to the check.

"Benny is a friend—I'd give him the shirt off my back. He'd wash it, iron it, and charge me a dollar.

"Jack is the only guy who'll get off at Albuquerque and sell blankets to the Indians.

"Here's a guy who came to California for arthritis forty years ago—and he's finally got it."

JACK CARTER: "Jack Benny is lucky to be here tonight. He was locked in a pay toilet at Kennedy Airport. Also, he has shingles—Mary caught him with a broad and the roof caved in."

BOB HOPE: "I don't want to say Benny is cheap, but the only time he'll pick up a check is when it's made out to him.

"During the war Jack was a dollar-a-year man. That's not what he got—that's what he spent.

"Remember the total eclipse of the sun? Jack ran over to the Western Union office to send a night letter."

GEORGIE JESSEL: "I've known Jack ever since I was a little boy. He used to hold me on his knee and tell me about his old friends William McKinley and Chester Arthur and Aaron Burr. Do you know what he did before he came here to get this honor? He went to visit his son in the old age home. Now isn't that nice?"

Georgie Jessel

Georgie Jessel, the Toastmaster General of the United States, has presided at almost every important dinner since anybody can remember.

Georgie insisted that I never pull my punch lines when I'm roasting him. I thought you might enjoy a combination of some of the dinners where Jessel sat still for the March of Dimes, the City of Hope, the State of Israel, and others, while his friends and colleagues used him for target practice for the sake of charity.

"Georgie Jessel," I started, "this year alone personally supported 1,250,000 Jews in Israel—and 325 chorus girls in the United States.

"In his honor we are going to plant an Arab in the lobby of the Actors Temple.

"I'm sorry that Jessel's latest girlfriend couldn't be here tonight, but her mother won't let her cross the streets by herself.

"His fiancée is now a counselor at camp, and he's so proud of her. He just got a letter from her—she just made the Boy Scouts."

125

JACK CARTER: "George is an unhappy man. He just got his first anti-Semitic letter—and it was in Yiddish."

GEORGE BURNS: "Jessel is so sentimental he cries at card tricks.

"Years ago Georgie Jessel was starring in *The Jazz Singer* on Broadway, and he was a sensation. But when Jack Warner made the picture of *The Jazz Singer*, who do you think starred in it—Al Jolson. Well, naturally this upset Jessel, and Georgie took an oath that he'd break Jack Warner if it cost him his last cent. Jack Warner doesn't know this but he's only got about two weeks to go, because Jessel's down to his last $120. If Jessel happens to meet a girl tonight, Warner will be broke tomorrow.

"While I'm on the subject of *The Jazz Singer*, I saw Jessel do it on Broadway, and you remember the story. The father is a cantor, and the son wouldn't follow in his footsteps. And at the finish of the play the father dies and the son gives up show business and comes into the synagogue and sings Kol Nidre. Well, this affected me very much. I felt like it was my life, because my father was a cantor. He wasn't exactly a full-time cantor, he was sort of like a disappointment act. In case a real cantor got sick, my father would take his place. I remember once during the high holidays a cantor got sick and they sent for my father. They said, 'Let's hear you sing something,' so my father sang. You know, that year the synagogue was closed on Rosh Hashanah.

"Well anyway, Jessel's performance in *The Jazz Singer* just took me apart, I cried like a baby. And when he finished Kol Nidre I ran backstage with the tears streaming down my face to congratulate him. But Jessel's publicity man, Bennett, was standing outside his dressing room and wouldn't let me in. He said, 'You can't go in, Jessel has all his clothes off.' I said, 'What's that got to do with it, I've seen a naked Jew before. I want to tell him how great he was.' Bennett said, 'Not now, he's got a girl in there who he's putting into show business."

JAN MURRAY: "What could I possibly say about our great guest of honor. There have been a lot of jokes tonight about Georgie and Israel, but we all know that most of Georgie's adult life, his energies and affections have always been divided in two places . . . his heart is always in Israel and his body is in a little love nest on Fifty-eighth Street.

"But it's common knowledge what Georgie has done for the glorious State of Israel. As you all know, one time it was just a desert, but he helped to plant trees, homes, hospitals, schools, and an airport. Can you imagine what he could have done if he didn't have a hernia?

"Look what this man has contributed to show business. Do you realize Georgie Jessel was the first comedian to do jazz songs on Broadway? He was the first comedian to use a telephone in monologue. But most important, he was the first comedian to be tried under the Mann Act. That was the time he carried Sophie Tucker over the state line. How do you think he got the hernia?

"That's right, my friends, this great human being has never changed. Even as a youngster he was what he is today . . . a dirty old man."

Cary Grant

GREGORY PECK started it by telling a story: A little old lady kept two monkeys for companions. These monkeys were the joy of the little old lady's life, but they finally died, almost at the same time. The old lady did not want to part with them forever, so she took them to the taxidermist. He said, "Would you like them mounted?" She said, "No, oh no, just holding hands."

GEORGE BURNS: "I want to put my cigar into my holder. At my age, this is exciting. I was in Adolph Zukor's office playing gin rummy with him. He knocked and said, 'I'm going down with ten.' He had a seven and a four. I said, 'Mr. Zukor, before we throw in the cards, I understand you are ready to do another picture with Cary Grant and Carole Lombard— sort of a comedy. Did you ever think of making a picture like that with Gracie and myself?' He said, 'George, you've been with Paramount for six years. Don't you like working with Paramount?' I said, 'I love it.' He said, 'Don't you like living in California?' I said, 'I love it.' He said, 'You wouldn't want to move back to New York.' I said, 'No, sir.' He said, 'How much is seven and four?' I said, 'Ten.' "

TOM BROKAW: "I was very nervous about being here tonight. But after reading the rundown list . . . They have the speakers right in order—it said 'HOWARD COSELL, Comedy,' 'Tom Brokaw, Talk.' If what Howard did qualifies as comedy, anything I do would qualify as talk."

RED BUTTONS came on screaming: "CARY GRANT is a man with heart—spends three hours a week in hospitals teaching nervous people how to eat Jell-O."

"A man with heart, who once took Ray Charles to a Marcel Marceau concert, but he wasn't happy with that—so he went to Stevie Wonder's house and rearranged his furniture."

"In Israel at an expedition of Hadassah housewives who believe that chicken soup can bring the Dead Sea back to life—the man was there. In New York City at a garment center luncheon for business partners who trust each other—the man was there."

Now he was hollering: "A dinner for Cary Grant? Adam—who said in the Garden of Eden, 'I've got more ribs—you got more broads?'—never got a dinner. Lot—who said when his wife was turned into a pillar of salt, 'Salt I got—popcorn I need.'—never got a dinner. Moses—who yelled when the Red Sea parted, 'What the hell is that—I was just going in for a dip'—never got a dinner. Noah's wife—who said to Noah, 'Please don't let the elephants watch the rabbits—never got a dinner. Amelia Earhart—who said, 'Stop looking for me—see if you can find my luggage'—never got a dinner."

Cary Grant's acceptance speech: "Two very elegantly dressed people were dancing in the ballroom. While they were dancing her necklace became undone. It fell down into the décolletage—the cleavage. She wriggled to try to free it, hoping it would go to the floor. It didn't. It got caught. She then said to her escort, 'Would you mind getting my necklace?' He said, 'How do you propose I do that?' She said, 'Put your hand down the back of my dress and get my necklace.' He put his

129

hand down the back of her dress, feeling around for it. All the other dancers stopped to watch this curious performance. He whispered in her ear, 'You know, I feel a perfect ass.' She said, 'Never mind the compliment—get the necklace.' "

Buddy Hackett

Roastmaster JAN MURRAY opened the evening: "I'm sure you'll understand when I tell you I've been looking forward to this evening about as much as I'd look forward to having my prostate examined by the Incredible Hulk.

"Buddy was offered a terrific deal to do a commercial for hemorrhoids, but he turned it down when they wouldn't give him creative control.

"One fast news item. Just came over the news. There was a hijacking this afternoon. They hijacked a bus filled with Japanese tourists. But thank God: They got over two million pictures of the hijackers.

MILTON BERLE: "SINATRA's my favorite Italian. I figured out why Italian guys have short necks. That's from standing before grand juries and saying, 'I don't know.'

"I'm seventy-eight years old, but feel like a twenty-year-old . . . unfortunately, there isn't one around.

"I've been married to Ruth for twenty-eight years. And now when I want to make love I have to go through what they call Jewish foreplay. That's three hours of begging.

"And then there's Italian foreplay: 'Marie, I'm home.'

"I have sex with Ruth almost every day of the week . . . almost Monday, almost Tuesday . . .

"I've tried everything to keep the flame of sex going. I redecorated the bedroom. Mirrors on the ceiling. Mirrors on the walls. Now I've got twelve different views of Ruth's headache.

"I told Ruth black underwear turns me on. So she didn't wash my shorts for three months.

"GEORGE BURNS was going to be here tonight, but last week he got an erection and he's waiting for the Crazy Glue to set.

"The first time I met Buddy Hackett, he knelt down and kissed my hand. Of course, at the time I was scratching my ass.

"Buddy and I were standing in the bar at the Concord Hotel and standing next to Buddy was a beautiful six-foot blonde. And this little guy had the chutzpah to look up at her and say, 'What do you say to a little fuck?' She said, 'Hello, little fuck.' "

"Buddy makes one television appearance a year and he suffers from overexposure."

FREDDIE ROMAN: "Thank you, Jan. I'm glad you mentioned your show *Treasure Hunt*. I was a big fan of *Treasure Hunt*. What no one knows is that it was invented by your wife, Toni, on your wedding night when she searched for your family jewels.

"MICKEY ROONEY was supposed to be Jan's cohost tonight,

but he's still celebrating the second anniversary of *Sugar Babies*, which is longer than he lasted with any of his wives.

"A lot of people wanted to be here tonight for Buddy, but couldn't make it. Mayor KOCH had to go to a FRANK PERDUE look-alike contest.

"A lot of people did show up. WARNER WOLF, who doesn't give a shit how much the subway fare goes up. He still goes under the turnstile anyway. ROGER GRIMSBY, one of the most influential men in all of television anywhere. He could probably make a girl a star overnight. I know because I heard him telling Miss Universe that just before the dinner started."

HENNY YOUNGMAN: "Last night I had a nightmare. I dreamed BO DEREK and my wife had a fight over me and my wife won.

"I'm glad to see MILTON BERLE here tonight. Milton was supposed to get a vasectomy, but the doctor said let sleeping dogs lie.

"I love the Italians. During World War II, an Italian girl saved my life. She hid me in a cellar. It was on Mulberry Street.

"I just found out why Jews don't drink. It interferes with our suffering.

"Last night Buddy met this gorgeous girl in a bar. After a few drinks she told him he could go as far as he wanted. So he drove her to Newark."

GENE BAYLOS: "I don't need this job tonight. In the winter I have another job. I smuggle Gentiles down to Fort Lauderdale.

"Did you hear the story about the fellow who came home and found his wife in bed with his best friend? He walked over to his friend and said, 'Sam, I have to, but you?'

"I want to tell you what three women of three different nationalities say while they are making love. The Italian woman says, 'Mama mia.' The French girl says, 'Ooh-la-la.' The Jewish girl says, 'Max, the ceiling has to get painted.'

"Newlyweds on their wedding night. The fellow says, 'Honey, tell me, am I the first man?' She says, 'Why does everybody ask me that?' "

JAN MURRAY was romantic for the finish: "We honor tonight one of the great men of the world—a man of understanding, principle, love, a man of dignity and human decency—but enough about the Pope.

"Now we get to Buddy Hackett. It's appropriate we give him a dinner—everybody does. When he picks up his own check, he's treating."

Buddy accepted it all nicely: "I'm not as good as you said, but I'm much better than you're thinking.

"I really don't deserve this—but I have a social disease, and I don't deserve that either."

Buddy said, "Thanks, thanks. I think the world of you all, and you know how screwed up the world is—and the same to you! I'd like to say something nice and loving to each and every one of you, but I just can't think of it."

Henry Kissinger

KIRK DOUGLAS, master of ceremonies: "We are hear to honor a man who has awakened in more Hilton hotels than ZSA ZSA GABOR.

"Of all his wondrous achievements, what I admire the most is that he has been appointed to the Nobel sperm bank. The mind boggles to think that in another generation any woman can go to any sperm bank in America and order a Henry Kissinger with an American accent.

"Henry Kissinger has been here for forty years and he sounds like he's arriving next Thursday.

"He's been taking dictation lessons from ABE HERSHFELD—who makes KHADAFY sound like an English professor.

"He is giving up politics to teach at Columbia University—Broken English."

BARBARA WALTERS: "I once asked Henry Kissinger how he felt when people called him a swinger. 'I love it,' he said. 'Now when I bore people they think it's their fault.'

"Henry Kissinger was once heard to remark upon an august occasion at which he was being honored by a group of dignitaries and celebrities, 'I haven't seen this impressive a group since the last time I found myself in Versailles at the Hall of Mirrors.' "

BOB HOPE: "This has been some marathon. I haven't spent a night like this since HOWARD COSELL invited me to his reading of the *Encyclopedia Brittanica.*

"I was the original Abbot of the Los Angeles Friars Club. A very responsible position. About as important as the dialogue director of *Deep Throat.*

"I can't wait to see RONALD REAGAN in the White House. An actor in the White House. With MAX FACTOR as head of the State Department. And I can see the ambassadors sending DON RICKLES, the ambassador, over to Iran. Don walks over to the Ayatollah and says, 'Look, Kakamami, you need a new flea collar.'

"I love this dais. I love WILLIAM F. BUCKLEY, the Phi Beta Kappa Don Rickles. I had a long discussion with him before the dinner. He was very impressed with me. He said I nodded in all the right places. In politics he's a middle-of-the-roader. He's somewhere between Barry Goldwater and Louis XIV. I wouldn't miss him on television. I watch him all the time. That's all I can do. I won't be able to understand him until they get subtitles.

"I've been with NBC for forty-two years. Twelve years on radio, selling Pepsodent in those days. Of course, most everyone I sold Pepsodent to is now using Polident.

"Henry Kissinger was graduated from Harvard summa cum laude and voted the highest honor—most likely to succeed . . . at Radcliffe.

"We will always be indebted to Henry Kissinger. He was the first man to get Israel and Egypt to agree on anything since Moses. He finally got Israel to drive back from the Suez Canal. But they drive a hard bargain. Miami Beach is now part of Israel.

"And since the settlement the Arabs and the Jews are getting along amazingly well. Last night OMAR SHARIF took MYRON COHEN out dancing.

"It isn't easy for Henry Kissinger to be domesticated. Last night Nancy asked him to take out the garbage and he took it to China.

"Even though he's out of office, even now the eyes and ears of the world are on Henry Kissinger. The other night Kissinger sprang a leak in his water bed and nearly drowned JACK ANDERSON."

HENRY KISSINGER: "A lot has been said tonight about my ego, which I frankly loudly resent. My wife, Nancy, doesn't agree with it. Neither does my dog, Tiber. Nor do my staff assistants, Matthew, Mark, Luke, and John.

"I'd like to clear up the unpleasantness regarding the controversy regarding my *60 Minutes* interview. I'm quoted as saying they were going to do a hatchet job. And that I was threatening to sue them. They claim I was seeking editorial control. It is all a terrible misunderstanding. *60 Minutes* is doing a program called 'The Shah/Kissinger Connection.' That I cannot accept. Anything that gives me second billing is a hatchet job. And I would never dream of threatening so defenseless a person as MIKE WALLACE.

"As for editing, all I asked for was that they must use complete sentences. They said they would allow me up to fourteen minutes. They did it to me right there . . . I don't have any sentences that go less than fifteen minutes.

"I asked **DAVE TEBET** what I should talk about tonight. And he said, 'Anything you want, pal.' So I decided to dispense with the usual boring late-night speech. I was tempted to give this audience something you would never forget . . . I decided to read my book to you. This room has no function again until next Thursday night. So I can get through it if I cut it by a third, which I can do if I drop the word 'I.'

"My second volume goes into some details of my background and upbringing. And it is in the great American tradition. And if I can just read one key paragraph: 'I was born in a log chalet . . . in the south Bourbon state of Bavaria, whose national hero was King Ludwig the Mad. When I was a boy I read Mitterand and other great Americans by the light of a kerosene lamp. The turning point in my life which set me on the road to politics occurred when I came across Lincoln's famous phrase, "You can fool some of the people all the time and all of the people some of the time . . ." Hey, I said to myself, those are pretty good odds.'

"The rest is the simple story of how I saved the world.

"The hour is late, but I must warn you I am about to take my seat and unless I hear tumultuous applause I will return to the podium and begin reading my book . . . in German."

Sophie Tucker

Unless you had heartburn, you don't remember every course at every dinner, whether at your mother-in-law's or if you're putting up one hundred bucks a shot at a Friars' roast. But there are some things over the years that do stick to the ribs.

Like the time the Friars skewered Sophie Tucker. The "Last of the Red Hot Mamas" was the first lady ever to get the golden shaft at the proverbial stag roast.

The Friars broke with tradition and honored Sophie on the celebration of her golden jubilee in show business, fifty years of great entertainment from a great lady. The year 1953 was a good year. On the dais surrounding the First Lady of the Friars were MILTON BERLE, GEORGIE JESSEL, FRANK SINATRA, SMITH AND DALE, JACK E. LEONARD, DEAN HARRY DELF, JESSE BLOCK, MYRON COHEN, ABEL GREEN, and EARL WILSON, besides BENNY FIELDS, JACK CARTER, RED BUTTONS, MEYER DAVIS, HENNY YOUNGMAN, and scores of other show-biz notables in the audience.

Sophie said, "This is the first time I've been in a room alone with enough men. The hell of it is, it comes so late."

It was FRANK SINATRA who said it all in a parody to Sophie, written by MILTON BERLE, to the tune of "Mother" ("Put them all together, they spell mother"):

S is for the sweetness that's within her.
O is for the oldies that she sings.
P is for the people that adore her.
H is for the happiness she brings
I is for the ideals that she lives by.
E is for her endless curtain calls.

Put them all together they spell Sophie
The only Friar without balls
And we're not certain
The only Friar without balls.

Phyllis Diller

BUDDY HACKETT was the head roaster: "Last year Phyllis snuck in dressed as a man. She did the whole thing and then she told every newspaper she was here. That afternoon I said to her husband, 'Let's make her the guest of honor next year.' He said, 'How do you think it will work?' I said, 'It will work. However, I want security so that no one sneaks in again as a man.' So, gentlemen, for a security check, I'd like for you to reach over to the man next to you and hold his balls throughout the luncheon.

"I've known Phyllis a long, long time, before she had a face lift, a boob job, a tummy tuck, and she taught herself how to tell jokes, laugh at them while she's talking through her ass at the same time."

JOEY ADAMS: "I was listening to you, Buddy, and I was worrying and preparing this afternoon's program. I was worrying about doing a joke with the word *navel* in it.

"A luncheon for Phyllis Diller is about as exciting as watching **BELLA ABZUG** getting undressed.

"I've known Phyllis Diller, man and boy, for forty years. I like her more as a man than I did as a boy. She's pretty tough, too. She's got more balls than any poolroom. And a tough gal. Her husband went to the ASPCA to get a divorce. He claimed his wife was a bitch. That's all I can tell you.

"Phyllis is proud of the fact that the police department put up her picture in all the jails in the country. They put the picture up to discourage sex offenders.

"Look at her body. On her chest is tattooed 'In case of rape, this side up.'

"The other day she ran into the police station and said, 'I've been raped by a Jew.' The cop said. 'How do you know he was Jewish?' She said, 'Because I had to help him.' "

"Phyllis Diller willed her body to science, but science is contesting the will.

"As a child she was abandoned by her parents and raised by wolves.

"This is a true story. When she was a baby her mother held her up to be kissed by a politician. The politician decided to avoid the race. He did not run.

"I'm not saying that Phyllis Diller is starved for sex, but she goes to a gynecologist once a week. She went to this gynecologist the other day and said, 'Will you examine me with two fingers please.' He said, 'Wait a minute. I've been a gynecologist for over forty years and never used more than one finger. Why do you want two fingers?' She said, 'I want a second opinion.'

"I'm sorry her best pal, MILTON BERLE, couldn't be here, but something came up and he was very proud.

"I was there when Milton and Phyllis were having a discussion. And as you know, Milton is supposed to be the best-endowed comedian, the best-endowed entertainer in America or anywhere. A guy walked over to Phyllis when she was talking to Milton and said to Milton, 'I'll bet you $1,000 mine is bigger than yours.' Phyllis said, 'I'll take that bet.' Then she said to Milton. 'Take out just enough to win.'

"To me it's a joy to be here with such great stars and to be in the same company to honor a great gal. I love her. I have no taste. But I love her."

DICK CAPRI: "You have to admit she looks great. She looks so good because her bust sags so much it pulls the wrinkles out of her face.

"Her gynecologist will only examine her by mail.

"It is true that the reason she left her husband, Fang, is because he was a schmuck. In fact, her last words to him were 'Fang, you're a schmuck. You've always been a schmuck. You are a schmuck now. You do schmucky things. You look like a schmuck. You dress like a schmuck. If they had a contest for schmucks, you'd come in second.' He said, 'Why second?' She said, 'Because you're a schmuck.' "

JIM BAILEY as Phyllis Diller: "I'm a mess. If the bags under my eyes get any bigger, I will have found a use for my old brassieres.

"I recently asked my doctor should I undergo a change of sex. He said, 'From what?'

"When I go to the beauty parlor it makes about as much sense as an ashtray on a motorcycle. I was down there today for a total of seven and a half hours—for the estimate. They don't like me to come in there. They have a special entrance for me, marked 'Emergency.' I always back out so they think

I'm leaving. And today I overheard them discussing mercy killing. That damn fairy hairdresser had the nerve to tell me my hair does not respond to gravity. I've got news for him, neither does he. His wrists are so limp his self-winding watch stopped three years ago. His roommate is even weirder. He sells toilet paper on Fire Island. He's known as Mary Queen of Scott's.

"I had a terrible thing happen to me last night—nothing. Actually, I got a hysterical call from a peeping Tom last night to lower my shades. He said he was eating.

"I went shopping to Macy's the other day. I said to the salesgirl, 'I'd like to see something cheap in a dress.' She said, 'The mirror is to the left.'

"I'm so tired of getting my bras back from the laundry marked 'Flatwork.' "

FOSTER BROOKS: "I remember a lot of things before I was even born. I remember going to a picnic with my father and coming home with my mother.

"Last time I went to see a doctor, he said, 'I'm afraid I've got some bad news for you.' I said, 'What's that?' He said, 'You could go anytime.' I said, 'That's not so bad—I haven't gone for four days.'

"He then said, 'I really have some bad news and some good news for you.' I said, 'OK, give me the bad news.' He said, 'Well, it's all how you regard something like this, but you show very definite signs of homosexuality.' I said, 'Oh come on. What in the world is the good news?' He said, 'The good news is I think you're cute.'

"Phyllis went out ice fishing with seven guys. Seven guys. And she came back with a red snapper.

"Fang was always complaining about Phyllis. Finally I said, 'What if you came home one night and you found Phyllis in bed with another man? What would you do first?' He said, 'I'd shoot his seeing-eye dog.' "

FREDDIE ROMAN: "Phyllis has had so many face lifts she has a little goatee."

JACK CARTER: "I want to thank my high-school pal, BUDDY HACKETT, and the Friars Club for flying me in from Los Angeles in such style. All my life I've wanted to fly People's Express. It's a great airline. Eighteen minutes before takeoff, the passengers get together and elect a pilot.

"I want to thank BILL WILLIAMS, FRANK SINATRA's afterbirth, for the wonderful room he got me here at this very chic hotel. Thin walls. I've been heard of hearing the couple next door, but seeing them?

"MILTON BERLE would have been here, but unfortunately he's in the hospital getting an erection bypass.

"FRANK SINATRA would have been here except for the distance. He's in the lobby.

"Phyllis ran away and went to Hollywood. She had no money, no funds, but she stayed at the best hotels—for an hour at a time. In fact, she was once raped. She didn't know it until the check bounced.

"Then she met Fang. They were introduced by a mutual friend—a bellhop."

PHYLLIS DILLER: "I can't tell you how it feels to be man of the year. I feel like Linda Lovelace with lockjaw.

"I loved JOEY ADAMS: I've watched him. He's a storyteller,

145

a raconteur. And for years I've watched his growth. He's having it removed next week.

"And he's getting on in years. He's so old he can remember a fight between two white guys.

"**FOSTER BROOKS** is having a rough time. His act is at the Betty Ford Clinic.

"**JACK CARTER** has the disposition of an old Hoover vacuum cleaner. It sucks.

"We invited my old college chum **HUGH DOWNS** here today to give this place a little class. It didn't work. Hugh is about as exciting as vapor lock. I'll tell you what he's like. He has a little black book, and next to **JOAN COLLINS**'s name he wrote, 'Has good posture and likes to bowl.'

"There was a hurricane named after me. Phyllis. Sagged over South Carolina."

"**JACKIE VERNON** flunked the dress code for K-Mart."

"My vocabulary today has been so enlarged that the next time I hit a truck driver. I'm going to fight back."

"**JIM BAILEY** went on the *Dating Game* and chose himself—and scored."

"I've had so many face lifts. If I have one more it'll be a Caesarean."

PART III

The Joey Adams
Roast Dictionary

Here come the jokes, folks. Study well before using then cut them down to your size before you cut them up—to fit your target.

This dictionary of roast lines will prepare you in case you face the doctor, lawyer, or businessman. I'll prepare you with lines when you attack the actor, philanthropist, comic, enemy or friend—rich man, poor man, beggar man, thief . . .

I'll prepare you for everything and anything but failure.

If you listen to me, I can make you the talker of the town. You know BERLE? He listened to me. GEORGE BURNS, great monologist? He listened to me. BOB HOPE listened to me. HENNY YOUNGMAN? He didn't listen!

A

ACCOUNTANT

This guy has the only office with recovery rooms.

I never try to fool the I.R.S.—I couldn't even fool my accountant. He laughed harder at my income tax returns than he does at my jokes.

But this is a fair accountant—he can come up with so many extra deductions that you'll wind up with enough money left over to post bail.

He's just written a new pamphlet, "30 Ways to Save on Your Taxes—And 50 Things to Do While You're in Jail."

My accountant told me, "In the event that a mistake is made on your tax returns, we will help negotiate the sale of rights to your prison memoirs."

A toast to a great accountant—someone who specializes in reading fiction.

One thing about my tax man. He's the type who could swim safely through shark-infested waters. No doubt he'd be given professional courtesy.

A tax accountant is a person who solves a problem you didn't know you had in a way you don't understand.

ACTOR

You can pick out an actor—by the glazed look that comes into their eyes when the conversation wanders away from themselves. I better mention his name or we'll lose him . . .

I love actors—I love _____ for his belief in God and himself—and I hope he'll forgive me for giving God top billing.

He has an alarm clock and a telephone that don't ring—they applaud.

He's lucky he doesn't have to pay taxes on what he thinks he's worth.

What a star. This guy so enjoys being in front of the lights, He volunteers for police line-ups.

Every time he looks in the mirror, he takes a bow.

He'll never get married—he can't find a woman who will love him as much as he does.

ADVERTISING

Doing business without advertising is like winking in the dark at a pretty girl—you know what you are doing but nobody else does.

To sell something, tell a woman it's bargain—tell a man it's deductible.

Talk about honest advertising: I saw this sign in the win-

dow of an antique shop: COME IN AND BUY WHAT YOUR GRAND-
MOTHER THREW AWAY.

There's one thing in this country I can't figure out: Streets
aren't safe, parks aren't safe, and subways aren't safe, but under our arms we have complete protection.

Advertising is 85 percent confusion and 15 percent com-
mission.

You can wear this suit in the rain. It shrinks, but you can
wear it in the rain.

Talk about progressive advertising: this department store
ad offered in a local New York paper, "Maternity dresses—
for the modern miss."

Advertising can make people live beyond their means—
but so can marriage.

AGE

He's so old, he doesn't learn history, he remembers it.

You know you're getting old when you go to a drive-in
movie and keep the seat belt fastened.

He's at the age now, when he goes out with a girl he can't
take yes for an answer.

He's at the age now when the battle of the sexes is none
of his affair.

Of course he's against sin—he's against anything he's too
old to enjoy.

153

Now that he's got money to burn, his pilot light went out.

He's got young blood, but he keeps it in an old container.

We tried to dig up friends who knew our guest of honor when he was young—and that's what we'd have to do, dig them up.

He's at the age now where his sex drive is in park.

He's at the age now where the only thing he can sink his teeth into is water.

When he goes to bed now, he turns out the light for economic reasons rather than romantic reasons.

He must be getting old—he decided to go to a disco the other night and they wouldn't admit him unless he was accompanied by a chiropractor.

He got an award from the President of the United States. It's one of the few Chester Arthur ever gave out.

He looks the same as he did twenty years ago. So does a dollar bill.

You've reached middle age when you know your way around but you'd rather not go.

I don't want to say he's old, but he reached the age of consent about 75,000 consents ago.

He's at the age when he has to use tenderizer on his Cream of Wheat.

If it wasn't for liver spots she'd have no complexion at all.

So old, the picture on his driver's license is by Van Gogh!

His palms used to get sweaty when he thought a girl would say no—now they get sweaty when he thinks she'll say yes.

He's arrived at the age where, if he drops $10 in the collection plate, it's not a contribution, it's an investment.

ANALYSIS

I went to a psychoanalyst for years, and it helped—now I get rejected by a much better class of girls.

"Yes," she explained to the analyst, "I'm a virgin—but I'm not a fanatic about it."

I realized after four years and $10,000 worth of analysis that if I'd had the $10,000 in the first place, I wouldn't have needed the analysis.

ASTRONAUTS

You think you got trouble? I know one astronaut who got on a scale and his fortune said: "Beware of long trips."

We'll really be in trouble if the astronauts form a union—like taxi drivers. Imagine having to pay them by the mile.

Two Jewish astronauts were talking. One said, "Forget the moon—everybody is going to the moon—we go direct to the sun." "But we can't go to the sun. If we get within thirteen million miles of the sun, we'll melt."
"OK—then we'll go at night."

When the astronauts found out they were allowed 110 pounds of recreational equipment, they requested Raquel Welch.

B

BACHELOR

He loves home-cooked meals—but he has a big choice of cooks.

As the widow said to the bachelor, "Take if from me—don't get married."

A bachelor is a guy who goes to work every morning from a different direction.

Never trust a husband too far—or a bachelor too near.

A bachelor past fifty is a remnant—there is no good material left in him.

A bachelor is a guy who doesn't have to leave a party when he starts having a good time.

Married man to good-looking bachelor: "How in the world have you managed to stay single so long?" Bachelor: "It's easy. Every time I look at television commercials I learn that women are anemic, have stringy hair and large pores, and overweight, and have rough hands."

WARREN BEATTY describes a bachelor as someone who occasionally wonders who would make the best wife—a blonde, brunette, or redhead. But he always comes to his senses in the end and remembers that it really doesn't matter what color the truck is if it's gonna run him over anyway.

A man who believes that one can live as cheaply as two.

If a man has both a savings account and a checking account, the chances are he's a bachelor.

My neighbor says he feels sorry for bachelors. What do they do for aggravation?

BANKERS

What we need in this country is a bank where you deposit a toaster and they give you money.

I don't trust banks with counting money. If bankers can count, why do they always have eight windows and two tellers?

The trouble with most banks is that the man who writes the advertising is not the same guy who lends you the money.

A local bank teller is worried, reports PAT COOPER. "The bank examiner's due tomorrow, and he's short two toasters and a set of dishes."

BIBLE

I'm the guy that didn't object to the *Reader's Digest* coming out with a condensed version of the Bible, although I was a bit surprised that in the story of Noah, instead of raining forty days and forty nights, the short version says it rained all weekend.

I did like the new version of Adam and Eve where it says they had to leave the Garden of Eden because it was going condo.

Now the story is out that God called his writers together. "Gentlemen, I have a big show on Mount Sinai and I need some material." One volunteered, "How about 'Thou shalt not steal'?" Another suggested, "Thou shalt not kill." A third said, "Thou shalt not—" God interrupted, "Wait. How many times have I told you I can't use one-liners."

BORE

He has never been bored himself—but he *is* a carrier.

We have two disapointments tonight—BOB HOPE couldn't make it—and he could.

Your wife leaves you to go home to *your* mother.

Your boss will give you a raise if you quit.

Your children interrupt you to do their homework.

You're invited to be an after-dinner speaker and everyone decides to have breakfast instead.

He's the only man who ever had a paternity suit filed against him by his own children.

BOSS

Today we take up the plight of the bosses. A businessman can't win nowadays. If he does something wrong, he's fined; if he does something right, he's taxed.

If you want to know how to run a business, ask a man who hasn't any.

One manufacturer cried to me, "Business is so bad, even the people who don't intend to pay aren't buying."

The applicant agreed the job sounded OK but he told the boss that the last place he worked paid more. The future employer asked, "Did they give you rest periods, life insurance, and vacations with pay?" He said, "Yes, and a thousand-dollar holiday bonus and all holidays off." The boss asked, "Then why did you leave?" He said, "The company went bankrupt."

"This is just a suggestion. You don't have to follow it unless you want to keep your job."

BUSINESSMAN

He's not a yes-man—when the boss says no, he says no too.

Some businessman: He represents YASSIR ARAFAT for shaving commercials.

Our guest of honor makes money the old-fashioned way—he steals it.

"My son is a good businessman," Mrs. Adler said proudly.

"He's so dedicated that he keeps his secretary near his bed is case he should get an idea during the night."

Sign in the window of a vacant store: WE UNDERSOLD EVERYBODY.

"I have a hundred suits," the cloak-and-suiter was bragging, "and they're all pending."

"I buy a piece of merchandise for one dollar and I sell it for four dollars—you think three percent is bad?"

The dress manufacturer sent this letter to one of his customers: "Dear Sir: After checking our records, we note that we have done more for you than your mother did—we've carried you for fifteen months."

Two business partners are conversing. "I can't understand why we're losing money," says one, "the President insists business is better than ever." Says the other, "Maybe he has a better location than we have."

To get 10 percent out of him you've got to be at least a fifty-fifty partner.

We're a nonprofit organization. We don't mean to be, but we are.

C

CELEBRITY

A celebrity is someone who works all his life to become famous enough to be recognized—then goes around in dark glasses so no one will know who he is.

A celebrity is somebody who is known by many people he's glad he doesn't know.

A person who's bored by the attentions of people who formerly snubbed him.

CHARITY

He's a great philanthropist and a great humanitarian—he's loved by everyone. If his wife finds out, she'll kill him.

I know one charity which collected $30 million—and doesn't even have a disease yet.

A philanthropist is a guy who gives away what he should be giving back.

As the rabbi said: "Let's give freely and generously of our income as reported to the I.R.S."

CHEAP

Cheap? He's the only guy I know who walks off airplanes carrying a doggy bag.

He works for the government as a dollar-a-year-man, and even out of that he manages to save a little.

He's waiting for the Bible to come out in paperback.

He's always the first to put his hand in his pocket—and the last to bring it out again.

He tries to make every dollar go as far as possible—and every girl, too.

He is so cheap that the only time he'll pick up a check is when it's made out to him.

He is saving all his toys for his second childhood.

This character is so cheap, his nurse told me he was mad because he got well before all the medicine was gone.

Cheap? He thinks he's treating when he pays his own check.

Cheap? The only thing he ever gave to charity was a couple of poor relations.

Cheap? Some dark night if you really want to scare him, don't say, "Reach for the sky!" Say, "Reach for the check!"

He believes in free love—he won't spend a cent on a date.

He's a man of rare gifts—he hasn't given one in years.

CHEATING

There's one hotel in town that't strictly for cheaters. In fact, when a couple registers, they sign in as Mr. and Mrs. To-Whom-It-May-Concern. One guy followed his wife there and he broke into the room and found her making love to his best friend. "You'll pay for this," he shouted. The friend said calmly, "Are you on American Express? I never leave home without it."

Two doctors talking: "I know you've been making love to my wife. What do you think of her?" The second doctor, says, "Don't you know?" The first says, "Yes, but I wanted a second opinion."

My neighbor confided in me, "I told my wife the truth. I told her I was seeing a psychiatrist. And she told me the truth. She is seeing a psychiatrist, two plumbers, and a bartender."

"Your Honor," she told the judge, "I want a divorce. My husband has been cheating on me. Just last night I was walking down Broadway when I saw him go into a movie with another woman." "Then why didn't you follow them into the theater to find out who she was? It may have been just a harmless coincidence. You should have gone in after them." "I would have, but the fellow I was with had already seen the picture."

A good man is hard to find—until the husband opens the closet door.

My neighbor saw this guy in front of his house jogging naked. "How come you're jogging without any clothes on?" he asked him. His answer was "Because you came home early."

An eighty-year-old gentleman went to the hospital for his annual checkup. The doctor examined him and said, "You won't live another week if you keep chasing women." The old boy said, "Don't be ridiculous, I'm as healthy as a bull." "I know," the doctor said, "one of the women is my wife!"

I am firmly against husbands and wives cheating. I am firmly against anything I can't do.

I don't know who said it. I think it was me. "Every man cheats—and he is honest only when he's discovered."

COLLEGE

The trouble with the college kids today is their sex habits. Too many youngsters start experimenting with their fingers crossed—which happens to be the wrong part.

They take only top students in this college—must have an A in Pot.

He is well informed about anything he doesn't have to study.

The mother went to see the analyst and asked, "Tell me— I got a daughter in college—she doesn't use drugs, she's not pregnant, she doesn't drink, she got the highest marks in her class, and she writes to us every day—where did we go right?"

My kid goes to an Ivy League college—now he can write on toilet walls in Latin.

The personnel manager looked over the application of the

college graduate: "I see you've never been in jail—didn't you take any interest in college activities?"

The old man was bragging: "My son just made the Yale picket team."

One way to stop a student protest movement is to make it a required course.

CONGRESS

Some men join the navy and see the world. Others just join Congress.

ERNEST BORGNINE says, "I don't understand why they say congressmen spend money like drunken sailors. Sailors spend their own money!"

It is the first nuthouse I've ever known that's run by the inmates.

If we play "Hail to the Chief" when the President makes an entrance, why can't Congress have its own song when it convenes: "Send in the Clowns."

Where a man gets up to speak and says nothing, nobody listens, and everybody disagrees.

CREDIT

A device that enables you to start at the bottom—and go into a hole.

My car has something that will last a lifetime—monthly payments.

These days, if somebody pays you in cash you get suspicious. You think maybe his credit is no good.

It's great to take a loan. At least you know somebody's gonna call you.

Education is a wonderful thing—if you couldn't sign your name, you'd have to pay cash.

We don't live within our income—it's all we can do to live within our credit.

CREDIT CARDS

The credit card bit has really gone crazy. The other night I saw a fella at a restaurant who wanted to pay cash. The wouldn't take it until he showed his American Express card and his driver's license.

Credit cards are what people use when they discover that money can't buy everything.

A credit card is a plastic IOU.

The advantage a credit card has over money is that it can be used over and over again.

D

DENTIST

All my dentist does is make appointments for me to see another dentist. I really don't know if he's a dentist or a booking agent.

The dentist said to his patient: "The bad news is you've got three cavities—the good news is your gold crowns have tripled in value."

Show me a man with a gold tooth and I'll show you someone who put his money where his mouth is.

I asked my dentist to put in a tooth to match my other teeth. He put in a tooth with four cavities.

The modern dentist lives up to his claim "It won't hurt a bit" till the bill arrives.

DIPLOMAT

A diplomat praises married life while he stays single.

A diplomat thinks twice before saying nothing.

A diplomat is a guy who can convince his wife she looks fat in a mink coat or vulgar in diamonds.

I asked one diplomat what his favorite color was and he said, "Plaid."

The definition of a diplomat: He talks interestingly for an hour and doesn't say anything. Or: It's the art of skating on thin ice without getting into deep water.

The ability to take something and act as though you were giving it away.

A diplomat is an honest man sent abroad to lie for his country.

The UN keeps the peace. In twenty-five years there has never been a war in the UN building.

Divorce has done more to promote peace than the UN.

Would you call the UN the Tower of Babble?

A diplomat's life centers around three things: protocol, alchohol, and Geritol.

A diplomat is a person who can be disarming even though his country isn't.

A smart diplomat never stands between a dog and a lamp-post.

DOCTOR

Some Doctor: He never used local anesthetic, only imported.

He's into acupuncture—at bars he's always sticking people for drinks.

Some Surgeon: He moonlights as a chef in a Japanese restaurant.

He's a specialist—that's a doctor whose patients can be ill only during office hours.

He's a great doctor—he put me on my feet in no time—made me sell my car to pay his bill.

I'm a little nervous about going to see a doctor when I realize that doctors are usually described as practicing.

My doctor sent me a get-well card and in it was a bill for $50,000.

I bought a used car from my doctor and I know it's in good shape. He told me he only used it to make house calls.

The doctor said to his patient, "I'm happy to say that the crisis is over—that is, if you've got the $600."

The patient told his doctor, "I don't smoke, drink, keep late hours, gamble, or fool around with girls." The doc said, "How can I cure you if you have nothing to give up?"

The patient told the doctor he had shingles—so the doc tried to sell him aluminum siding.

The nurse at the hospital said to the patient, "You're just what the doctor ordered—a patient with a good credit rating."

DRINKER

They say drinking interferes with your sex life, but with this guy it's the other way around.

Go over to the brewery—and have them put a head on you.

He's in the same condition as the Great Wall of China—stoned.

Liquor may not be the world' greatest medicine, but at least you can order it without a prescription.

His doctor told him he had to eat more—so now he has three olives with his martini.

He's thinking of quitting—he's beginning to see the handwriting on the floor.

He drinks only on special occasions—like when somebody else is buying.

He's finally solved his drinking problem—now he wears an old suit in case he falls down.

He cut his finger. It's the first time I ever saw blood with a head on it.

DULL

This actor was so dull he was upstaged by the scenery.

He's so dull he could go on color TV and come out in black-and-white.

His life is so dull he looks forward to dentist appointments.

He died at twenty but he was buried at seventy.

You take him with you when you want to be alone.

A person who has nothing to say—and says it.

One who insists upon talking about himself when you want to talk about yourself.

DUMB-DUMBS

Dumb politician? He lost the election when he asked the Greenwich Village voters to follow a straight ticket.

Dumb? It takes him an hour and a half to watch *60 Minutes.*

If he said what he thought, he'd be speechless.

This dumb-dumb got a gold medal in the Olympics and had it bronzed.

He signs his checks on a typewriter.

If there's an idea in his head, it's in solitary confinement.

He was given a book for his birthday and is still looking for a place to put in the batteries.

E

EGOTIST

Conceited? His greatest concern is whether there is room for one more on Mount Rushmore.

Ego? He's writing a book: *Famous Men Who Have Known Me*.

His wife adores him—and so does he.

Talk about vanity: He cut his name out of the telephone directory and put it in his scrapbook.

He's so stuck on himself, he even signs his name to anonymous letters.

He likes you to come out and say what you think—when you agree with him.

Is he an egotist? He joined the navy so the world could see him.

He's carried on a great love affair for a long time—unassisted.

He gave up reading books—he found it took his mind off himself.

EXECUTIVE

A good executive is a man who will share the credit with the man who did all the work.

He doesn't believe in wasting time with secretaries. He uses the old saying, "If at first you don't succeed—fire her."

He's the perfect executive—when he's dictating to his secretary, he always ends a sentence with a proposition.

F

FASHION

Women's clothes are getting more masculine and men's clothes are getting more feminine. Pretty soon you'll be able to save a fortune by marrying someone your own size.

Girls' jeans will come in three sizes this year: small, medium, and don't bend over.

My neighbor's wife always wants to buy a new outfit every time they're invited out. He thought he'd play a big joke on her once and accepted an invite to a nudist wedding. The joke was on him. She spent $1,500 on a body lift.

CINDY notes, "I saw some of those new bikini fashions. Why, I have earrings that cover more than that."

Note to women who wear slacks: Does your end justify your jeans?

G

GAMBLING

They say that every election is a gamble, which is ridiculous—when you gamble, at least you have a chance to win.

I love to gamble, but I just can't throw my money around on gambling and drinking and women—I've got a government to support.

I just heard a touching story. There's a bookie down the street who changed his name to "Red Cross"—just so his customers' losses would be tax-deductible.

Las Vegas: Now there's a town for my money. They got some pretty classy hotels there—you have to wear a tie to lose your shirt.

A gambler goes to Atlantic City once a month to visit his money and leave a little interest.

He told me: "I learned how to leave Atlantic City with a small fortune—go there with a big one."

He tells me he had the best system for beating them at the crap tables—but then the casino opened.

GOLFER

The only time a golfer tells the truth is when he calls another golfer a liar.

If you break one hundred, watch your golf. If you break eighty, watch your business.

I found something that can take five points off your game—an eraser.

BOB HOPE praised JACKIE GLEASON's golf prowess. "He can putt and drive like a champ. In fact, he can do everything but bend over and tee up the ball."

The man said, "My wife told me, either I sell my golf clubs or we get a divorce. I'm going to miss her."

Golf has made more liars out of the American people than the income tax has.

He said, "I'm thinking of giving up golf—I can't break ninety even when I cheat."

RONALD REAGAN is the only President who is not a golf freak. "I was going to take it up again," he told me, "but you can't get your horse on the golf course." I asked, "What's your handicap? He said, "The Congress."

TIP O'NEIL is another who's not a golf nut. The way he's built, he has to putt from memory.

As one congressman said, "Playing golf gives us an opportunity to practice our lying."

177

GOSSIP

Hear no evil, see no evil, speak no evil—and you'll never be a success at a cocktail party.

Don't talk about yourself. It'll be done when you leave.

A gossip is a person who will never tell a lie if the truth will do as much damage.

H

HECKLER

The show-business fraternity has left longer-lasting scars on hecklers than Zorro. Every circle has a square who is "funnier than the guy on stage" until the guy on stage puts him back in the woodwork where he belongs. So if you're heckled on stage or at a party or at work, don't get angry—get funny.

I don't know what I'd do without you, but I'm willing to try.

There's a bus leaving in ten minutes—get under it.

Find yourself a home in a wastebasket.

If you had your life to live over again, don't do it.

Do you have a chip on your shoulder—or is that your head?

Someday you'll go too far, and I hope you stay there.

I won't ask you to act like a human being. I know you couldn't do imitations.

In your case brain surgery would be a minor operation.

One good way to save face is to keep the lower half shut.

If you have something to say—shut up.

Sir, you are annoying the man I love.

Sir, someday you'll find yourself—and will you be disappointed.

Why don't you phone me sometime so I can hang up on you.

If you're ever in California, sir, I do hope you'll come by my house and use my pool—I'd like to give you some drowning lessons.

You have a nice personality—but not for a human being.

HYPOCHONDRIAC

The hypochondriac was crying to the doctor that he had a fatal liver disease. "That's silly," the doctor explained. "How would you know? With that disease there is no discomfort of any kind." "My symptoms exactly."

He won't kiss a girl unless her lipstick has penicillin in it.

It's easy to spot a hypochondriac. He's the guy who can read his doctor's handwriting.

I

INFLATION

The young housewife picked out three apples, an orange, two pears, and a banana and handed them to the grocery clerk. "That'll be $4.75," he barked. She handed him a five-dollar bill and started to walk out. "Wait, you forgot your change," he called to her. "That's OK," she said sweetly. "I stepped on a grape on the way in."

I shop at a friendly grocer. They not only deliver, they arrange financing.

We're told that money isn't everything. The way things are going, soon it won't be anything.

Even inflation has its bright side. Now there's hardly enough candy in a five-cent candy bar to be fattening.

I wanted to join an organization that fights inflation—but they raised their dues.

We have the highest standard of living in the world. Too bad we can't afford it.

Sign in supermarket: NOBODY UNDER $21 ADMITTED.

INSULTS

You know, I'm forming an attachment for you—it fits rights over your mouth.

DON RICKLES blasted a ringsider: "The schnook wears a wash-and-wear suit—and gets a gravy stain on his silk tie."

If there's ever a price on your head, take it.

You have a ready wit—let me know when it's ready.

GROUCHO: I never forget a face—but in your case I'll make an exception.

DON RICKLES saw ERNEST BORGNINE in his audience and yelled, "Look at that face! Quick, call up Allstate—I think I've found an accident."

Don't get such a big head. Remember, even a pair of shoe trees can fill your shoes.

Wife: "When I was sixteen I was chosen Miss America." Husband: "In those days there were very few Americans."

Go jump in the ocean and pull a wave over your head.

Find yourself a home in a wastebasket.

There's a girl I would like to take home to mother—*her* mother.

INSURANCE

Life insurance is a system that keeps you poor so you can die rich.

I have a very reliable insurance company. In all the fifteen years they've insured me, they never missed sending me a bill.

"But, lady, you can't collect the life insurance on your husband—he isn't dead yet." "I know that—but there's no life left in him."

My car had a fifty-dollar debatable policy.

My father-in-law is in the insurance business. He sold me a twenty-year-retirement policy—at the end of twenty years, he retires.

He sold me group insurance—but the whole group has to get sick before I collect.

L

LABOR

Nobody wants to make house calls anymore. I called an exterminator to ask if he could kill roaches and he said, "Sure. When can you bring them over?"

The unions are fighting for a four-day week. What's the fight? Most workers are already working a four-day week—only it takes them five days to do it.

"Learn a trade," his father told him, "then you'll be able to go out on strike."

There was a postal strike—and nobody could tell the difference.

The union boss was telling his kid a bedtime story: "Once upon a time-and-a-half . . ."

I dropped a quarter down the sink and had to pay the plumber twenty dollars to get it back.

In union there is strength—but in unions even more strength.

When it comes to top qualifications, it's hard to beat having a father who owns the company.

LAWYER

If you can't get a lawyer who knows the law, get one who knows the judge.

His father is Catholic, his mother is Jewish—when he goes to confession, he bring his lawyer along.

The lawyer was walking down Fifth Avenue when he saw two cars collide. He rushed over and yelled, "I'm a lawyer— I saw the whole thing—and I'll take either side."

Some men inherit money, some earn it, and some are lawyers.

The woman said, "I want something to calm my nerves." He said, "But I'm a lawyer, not a doctor." She said, "I know. I want a divorce."

Divorces are arranged so lawyers can live happily ever after.

A lawyer is a person who helps you get what's coming to him.

A lawyer saves your business and your estate from your opponents and keeps it for himself.

LAZY

He always goes through a revolving door on somebody else's push.

He bought a book on exercise and then lay down on the couch to read it.

The lazy bank robber made carbon copies of his holdup note.

When he leaves his house, he finds out which way the wind is blowing and goes that way.

Coffee doesn't keep him awake—even if it's hot and being spilled on him.

He could fall asleep in the middle of a nap.

He even takes a sleeping pill the first thing in the morning.

LIAR

He doesn't really lie, actually—he merely presents the truth in such a way that nobody recognizes it.

You can't believe him even if he swears he's lying.

I never knew a lawyer to lie—unless it was absolutely necessary.

He tells more lies than a girdle.

"Have you seen one of those instruments that detects falsehoods?" "Seen one? I married one."

If George Washington never told a lie, how come he got elected?

LOSER

A real loser is a guy who would marry BO DEREK for her money.

An accordion player in a topless girl band.

Talking about losers, have you been to Atlantic City lately? My neighbor loses money on the stamp machines. He plays cards and bets on horses just for laughs—he's already laughed away his bank account and his car. When his bookie's place burned down, the only thing the fireman saved were his IOU's. He bet on the horses that he was told would walk in—the only trouble was, the other horses ran.

He's such a loser, he gets cavities in false teeth.

I won't say he's a deadbeat, but the electric company bills him daily.

I'm the kind of guy whose twin sister forgets my birthday. I got married and wasn't in any of the wedding pictures. I set the house on fire when I was a kid and I was sent to my room.

A loser is a guy who wrecks his automobile while driving home from the bank after making his final car payment.

My secretary told me, "I guess I'm the kind of girl who just can't do anything right. Last week I kissed a prince and he changed into a frog."

M

MARRIAGE

He went home and gave his wife a good listening to.

PAT COOPER says: "I'm one of the silent majority—I'm married."

The wife said to her husband, "You know, you swore at me in your sleep last night." The husband answered: "Who was sleeping?"

When a man and woman marry they become one. The trouble starts when they try to decide which one.

MONEY

There are more important things than money—but women won't date you if you don't have any.

You never know the real value of money until you try to borrow some.

Money isn't everything—but it's mighty handy if you don't have a credit card.

The guy who said money isn't everything was almost right—it's nothing.

The trouble with finances today is that when you're rich it's usually on paper and when you're broke it's in cash.

They say money isn't everything. It won't buy health, it won't buy happiness, and it won't buy love. I say, give me the money and I'll rent them!

The wife was crying to her mother, "We always have too much month left at the end of our money."

A dollar these days will go further than you think. In fact, you can carry it around for days without finding anything you can buy with it.

MUSIC

He has plenty of music in him—he just can't get it out.

Some girls are music lovers—others can love without it.

If you want to remember his voice, tear a rag.

He's one of the finest musicians in the country—in the city not so hot.

He's a true musician—when he hears a lady singing in the bathtub, he puts his ear to the keyhole.

P

PLAYBOY

If he was living in a harem, he'd still have a girl on the outside with whom he'd be cheating.

The fastest worker I ever knew was a man who rushed up to a girl and said, "I'm a stranger in town. Direct me to your flat."

He has a good head on his shoulders—but it's a different one every night.

Playboy to playgirl at a party: "You look like the outdoor type—let's go out in the bushes."

When a girl says no to his proposal, he holds her for further questioning.

PLAYGIRL

She's crossed more state lines than Greyhound.

She only looks for one thing in a man—a rich father.

Will Rogers once said, "I never met a man I didn't like." I've got a girl who feels the same way.

I have a friend who once lived in a house of ill repute for about three months. It wasn't too fancy a place, but what room service!

Did you ever get mixed up with a German call girl? When they call, you better listen.

The delicious blonde was telling her psychiatrist the problem: "Whenever I have a drink, Doctor, I want to make violent love to the first man I see." "Don't worry," said the psychiatrist, "as soon as I've mixed this cocktail we can sit down and discuss it."

POLITICS

There are two sides to every question—and a good politician takes both.

All politician give the same advice: "Always be sincere, whether you mean it or not."

He grew up to be a big-time pol—you can't believe him even when he swears he's lying.

RONALD REAGAN is not a typical politician because he doesn't know how to lie, cheat, and steal. He always had an agent for that.

You can always tell if a politician is telling the truth or not—if his lips are moving, he's lying.

A sincere politician will never tell a lie—if the truth will cause more damage.

One thing about the senator—when he makes up his mind, he's full of indecision.

If he goes to Washington, he'll double-cross the Potomac.

Every politician is out to make a name for himself. Most of those names can't be printed in a family newspaper.

HENRY KISSINGER says: "Why do they say that politics makes strange bedfellows? How about prostitution!" Come to think of it—it's the same thing.

I know a congressman who was so unpopular that he ran unopposed and lost.

PREPARED

1. Be funny. Leave the preaching to the rabbi, priest, or minister. Win your argument with a funny story instead of a sad one.

2. Be prepared. Don't be caught with your gags down and your mouth open without anything to say.

3. Use the joke or the gag that fits and fits you.

4. Practice. Every day. On the butcher, the baker, or the candlestick maker's wife.

5. Personalize your stories. Name the characters and the place.

6. Be brief. The mind cannot accept what the seat cannot endure.

7. Laugh at yourself. Use yourself or your family as the butt.

8. Use the gag file to find the subject or the jokes you want and then apply it to your target.

9. Switch the gag if necessary to give it a custom fit.

10. Memorize the "savers"; they may save you from sure death.

PSYCHIATRIST

The shrink told his patient, "The trouble with you, Max, is you don't relax—you take your troubles to bed with you." He said, "What do you want me to do? My wife refuses to sleep alone!"

Anybody who goes to see a psychiatrist should have his head examined.

The profession that has raised the proverbial "penny for your thoughts" to over $50 an hour.

A psychiatrist is a talent scout for a nuthouse.

A good shrink goes to a strip show and watches the audience.

I told my analyst that everyone's always rushing me. He told me my hour was up.

I told my psychiatrist, "I'm always forgetting things—what should I do?" He said, "Pay me in advance."

A psychiatrist is a doctor some people go to slightly cracked and leave completely broke.

PUT-DOWNS

He goes with this girl, Sylvia. Everybody says she's a ten, but I happen to know she charges twenty.

He willed his body to science and science contested the will.

He's not too swift. He's the kind who would steal a car and keep up the payments.

Our guest of honor is a humble and modest man—and with good reason.

He has never been bored himself—but he is a carrier.

I have not known our guest of honor long, but I know him as long as I intend to.

To him a woman's body is a temple, and he tries to attend services as often as possible.

The trouble with business today is, when you're rich it's on paper; when you're poor, it's cash.

Don't trust anything he says while he's in love, drunk, or running for office.

He's the inventor of the do-it-yourself massage parlor.

He gives a lot of money to the church. It's called Our Lady of the Tax Shelter.

He has the body of an eighteen-year-old—waiting for him in the car.

The only sex life he has is when his doctor tells him to cough.

Our guest of honor has an unlisted phone, a numbered bank account, and a post office mailing address, which is all unnecessary because nobody really wants to reach him in the first place.

He's not a bad guy until you get to know him.

R

RELIGION

Our guest of honor is so religious he has stained-glass spectacles.

His Eminence JOHN CARDINAL O'CONNOR wants to be treated like any other guest. He laughed loudest when I said at one Catholic dinner, "About the pill, your Eminence—if you don't play the game, don't make the rules."

I better not do my religious jokes here tonight. The last time I did was at a dinner for the cardinal—that was a year ago, and I haven't won at bingo since.

Our guest of honor suggested having a drive-in confessional with a huge red-and-green neon sign reading: STOP AND TELL—OR GO TO HELL.

He tells me so many are going back to religion, Dial-a-prayer just added three more numbers.

He's a very religious man—he worships himself.

He thinks high cholesterol is a religious holiday.

Las Vegas is the most religious city in the world—at any hour you can walk into a casino and hear someone say, "Oh, my God!"

My wife is so Catholic we can't get fire insurarnce—too many candles in our house.

Hollywood Catholics are different—they're the only Catholics who give up matzo balls for Lent.

His father is Catholics, his mother is Jewish—when he goes to confession, he brings his lawyer along.

RICH

He's so rich he's got money to burn. Why not? It's cheaper than gas.

He's so rich he just had his gums capped.

A rich man is an alcoholic—a poor man is a drunk.

Now that he's rich enough to afford to lose golf balls, he can't hit them far enough to lose them.

He is so rich, he cashed a check and the bank bounced.

Believe me, money isn't everything—a man with three million can be just as happy as a man with five million.

Money doesn't buy everything—but it puts you in a better bargaining position.

You can't see his hidden charms—his money is in Swiss banks.

This guy is so rich he has an unlisted wife.

He is so rich he has an unlisted number at Sing Sing.

It is better to live rich than die rich.

They really know how to live. They had a picnic, and even the paper plates were sterling silver.

It doesn't matter if you're born poor and you die poor—as long as you're rich in between.

I won't say he's one of the idle rich, but when he was little he used to hire another kid to do his coloring books.

Rich? Instead of wearing glasses when he drives, he has a prescription windshield.

How easy it is for a man to die rich, if he will but be contented to live miserable.

ROMANCE

At twenty-one you believe in long engagements. At forty-one you don't even believe in long introductions.

The best way to prove girls are dynamite is to try to drop one.

BURT REYNOLDS says, "I prefer a girl who's sexy, not brainy. When I feel intellectual I can always go to the public library."

She was telling her friend, "Not only did the wise guy run out of gas—he had a trailer with him!"

"I'm sure you'll like Charlie," she said to her father. "He's a very nice boy." Pop asked, "Does he have any money?" She replied, "Oh, you men are all alike. Charlie asked the same thing about you."

STEVEN KESSLER said it: "There are two times in life a woman is looking for the right man: when she's single and later on when she's got an unmarried daughter."

From the sexy mouth of **JOE NAMATH:** "They say a miss is as good as a mile, but I'm not so sure. After all, you can have a lot of fun with a miss, but what are you going to do with a mile?"

BURT REYNOLDS doesn't give a second thought to women. His first thought covers everything.

ZSA ZSA explains, "There's really nothing wrong with a woman welcoming all men's advances, darling, as long as they are in cash."

S

SAVERS

If the gags or jokes aren't doing to well here are some savers.

HENNY YOUNGMAN defuses his bombs with "I want to thank you for coming to my funeral."

MILTON BERLE: "Ever get the feeling you're in the wrong business?"

BOB HOPE: "Please come back to see me again, but not as a group."

My favorite saver, the one that never fails, is the sympathy line. "I have a little boy at home who is all alone. I'm the only one he has in the whole world. And when I come home at night, he rushes up to me and says, 'Daddy, were you a big hit tonight? Did they laugh, Daddy? Did they, huh?' And if I have to tell him I was a flop, it would break his heart. So your laughs and your applause and maybe a standing ovation are not for me, really, they're for that poor little kid who is sitting at home alone, just waiting to hear how I did tonight."

"Ya bum," one heckler screamed at DON RICKLES, "I'll put you in my back pocket." Don said, "Then you'll have more brains in your pocket than you have in your head."

MILTON BERLE was challenged by a small-timer at the Carnegie Delicatessen. "You want to have a battle of wits?" Miltie asked, "I'll check my brains and we'll start even."

Some comics have built their act on savers: "I started at the bottom, and after this show I'll stay there!"

"Is this an audience or a jury?"

"My mother said I would come out on top. She's right—I'm getting bald!"

"Before I came out here I was a comer. Now I'm a goner."

Is it a particularly quiet audience, especially after your best gag? "What time do you want to be called in the morning?"

Are you really in trouble? "I don't have to do this for a living. I could always starve!"

Savers can change disaster into victory. When a joke goes wrong: "We will now pause for thirty seconds of silence for that joke that just died."

SAYINGS

To err is human. To blame it on the other guy is politics.

There's only one way to handle a woman. But nobody knows what it is.

The best things in life are free. No wonder they are never advertised.

Save your money. Someday it may be worth something.

Advice to the loveworn: When wine, women, and song become too much for you, give up singing.

Marriage is wonderful. Without it husbands and wives would have to fight with perfect strangers.

Marriage is great. It's the living together that's tough.

Give a woman an inch, and immediately the whole family is on a diet.

A genius is one who can do anything but make a living.

There are two sides to every question—and a good politician takes both.

A word to the wise is sufficient: If you cheat on a diet, you gain in the end.

Eat, drink, and be merry—for tomorrow you diet.

It's tough to win. If you do something wrong, you're fined. If you do something right, you're taxed.

To find the secret of your youth, lie about your age.

Be kind to your friends. If it weren't for them, you'd be a total stranger.

Candy is dandy, but sex doesn't rot your teeth.

Cure virginity.

Chastity is its own punishment.

Support free enterprise—legalize prostitution.

Save water. Bathe with friends.

Don't marry for money. You can borrow it cheaper.

There are more things in life than money. There are also credit cards and overdrafts.

People who think they know everything always annoy those of us who do.

SEX

Sex is a big topic for the comics—especially the ladies. Gone are the days when the little woman was seen and not heard. Today, she's obscene and heard pretty well. Take mighty mouth JOAN RIVERS: "Sex with love is about the most beautiful thing there is; but sex without love isn't so bad either."

PHYLLIS DILLER says, "What sex life? I went to the Virgin Islands and they gave me a hero's welcome."

MARILYN SOKOL confides, "Men are after one thing, and one thing only, and for that I say, hallelujah!"

ARLENE DAHL: "The reason I don't make movies today is that in the old days actresses used to play parts. Now they reveal them."

Enjoy the sex act before Congress repeals it.

If you can't give up sex, get married and taper off.

203

Sex is good for you, and you don't need batteries.

There are a lot of things I don't understand. Like Dr. Reuben's book, *Everything You Always Wanted to Know About Sex.* The only thing is, he left out the most important part—where to get it.

CHEVY CHASE said, "My doctor told my wife and I that we should enjoy sex every night—now we'll never see each other."

EVA GABOR said it: "If you are going to wear the pants in your family, then your husband's mistress will wear the diamonds."

SHORT

I've always wanted to be on a dais with him—because I admire a man who could walk into a limo without bending down.

He's so little, he saves a lot of money—he walks under the turnstiles in the subway.

He is short and superstitious—this morning he walked under a black cat.

She was so short that when she wore a mini-skirt the hem got dirty.

When he sits down and stands up he's the same size.

He was so small and she was so tall, when he wanted to make love to her somebody had to put him up to it.

He was so short when he stood up, he looked like he was standing in a foxhole.

SMILE

A smile is the shortest distance between two people.

PHYLLIS DILLER explained why she smiles a lot: "My teeth are the only things I have that aren't wrinkled."

SQUELCHES

I don't know what makes you tick, but I hope it's a time bomb.

I couldn't warm up to you if we were cremated together.

Don't you ever get tired of having yourself around?

Next time you pass my house, I'll appreciate it.

Why don't you leave and let live?

The last time I met you was in a nightmare.

There's a biblical quotation, "Judas went out and hanged himself." And there's another: "Go thou and do likewise."

I don't know what I'd do without you, but I'd rather.

Stay with me—I want to be alone.

According to the theory of evolution, we're descended from either birds or monkeys. I don't see any feathers on you.

I'll swear eternal friendship for anyone who dislikes you as much as I do.

Don't go away—I want to forget you exactly as you are.

Brains aren't everything. In fact, in you're case they're nothing.

Let's play horse. I'll be the front end and you just be yourself.

THELMA LEE was heckled by a bore who yelled, "Hey, baby, take off your clothes." She squelched him with a line from *Kismet:* "Don't work up an appetite if you have no teeth."

I won't ask you to act like a human being. I know you couldn't do imitations.

Say, you're a regular CPA—a constant pain in the ass.

The old actor was boring his youthful listeners at the Friars Club. "Why," he exclaimed, "when I walked onstage the audience sat there open-mouthed." "You mean they all yawned at once?"

She: "You don't love me anymore. I'm going back to Mother." He: "Don't bother—I'll go back to my wife."

A: "Kiss my ass." B: "OK, but better mark the spot—you look all ass to me."

STOCKBROKER

Wall Street just voted him man of the year. Unfortunately the year was 1929.

He is always ready to back his judgment with your last dollar.

A stock market investor is someone who is alert, informed, attuned to the economic heartbeat of America—and cries a lot.

Some broker: He sold me a stock at six—and it went down twelve points.

This broker is really in trouble—he has a wife, a girlfriend, and a ticker—and they're all late.

They say the institutions are buying—directors or inmates?

He made a killing in the market—he shot his brother.

What we need is a little encouragement in the market. Not people calling it the "Down-Jones" average.

The big thing on Wall Street today are these investment clubs. Do you know what an investment club is? It's a way to lose money legally by a board of bookmakers.

T

TAXES

I dreamed that I saw a beautiful rainbow and started walking in search of the end of it. And when I came to the end of the rainbow, there really was a pot of gold there! And standing right next to the pot of gold was an I.R.S. agent!

I feel like writing a letter to the income tax bureau and telling them I can no longer afford their service.

After filing my income tax returns for this year, the only thing I expect to get back from the I.R.S. is an audit.

My revenue agent told me, "Listen, we sympathize with your problems, but the thing is, they won't fit in a computer."

One guy wrote the tax boys, "If this is a free country, how come I can't afford it?"

A taxpayer called the I.R.S. to ask if he could take a certain deduction on his income tax. The answer was "No!" followed by "This is a recorded announcement."

U

UGLY

Ugly is beautiful if you laugh at it:

Dr. JEFFREY GURIAN said: "I know I'm ugly—when I go to the airport, customs checks the bags under my eyes."

You ought to have your face capped.

His mother said her childbirth was painless—until she got her first look at him.

I took a Polaroid of him—the camera refused to develop it.

When she kisses him she closes her eyes—she has to.

He doesn't have any enemies—but his friends won't be seen with him.

She had her face lifted so many times, it's out of focus.

She looks like a professional blind date.

She has everything a man desires—muscles and a beard.

Their kids are so ugly, they didn't keep the pictures in the family album—just the negatives.

She came in third in a beauty contest—and she was the only one entered.

She has the perfect method for birth control—her face.

W

WOMEN'S LIB

The husband lectured his wife: "Stick to your washing, ironing, scrubbing, and cooking. No wife of mine is going to work."

Women's lib is opening the door for a lady and standing aside so she can rush in and take the job you're after.

I'm glad my wife joined women's lib—now she complains about all men, not just me.

Nowadays, if a woman says she sits around all day talking to her plants, it could mean her electronic plant in Pennsylvania and her textile plant in New York.

Woman was made from man's ribs, which any butcher will tell you isn't the best cut.

JOYCE BROTHERS notes: "God made man. Then he stepped back, looked, and said, 'I can do better than that!' "

GLORIA STEINNEM preaches, "Once upon a time, a liberated woman was someone who had sex before marriage and a job afterward."

As my neighbor said to his wife: "For the last time, absolutely not! No wife of mine is ever going to stop working!"

ROAST
of the
TOWN

Women who seek equal rights with men lack ambition.

I'm for women's lib, but I think too many girls get married before they can adequately support a husband.